THE MYSTERY OF GOD

F. M. GENUYT, O.P.

THE
MYSTERY
OF GOD

Translated from the French
by
JOHN J. PILCH, O.F.M

DESCLEE COMPANY
NEW YORK

Originally published in French under the title *Le Mystère de Dieu* in the series "Le Mystère Chrétien" (Paris and Tournai, Belgium: Desclée, 1963), this English translation is based on the current revised French edition.

Nihil obstat: Edward J. Montano, Censor librorum

Imprimatur: Terence J. Cooke, D. D., Archbishop of New York. August 8, 1968, New York, N. Y.

Library of Congress Catalog Card Number: 68-54220

Printed in Belgium

TABLE OF CONTENTS

TABLE OF THESES   xi

LIST OF ABBREVIATIONS   xv

GENERAL BIBLIOGRAPHY   xvii

INTRODUCTION   1

§ I.   *Theology and Theodicy*   1
     1. Faith, the source of theology   1
     2. Faith and demonstration   3
     3. Faith, knowledge of salvation   3

§ II.   *Natural and Supernatural Manifestation of God*   4

§ III. *The Possibility of a Natural Knowledge of God as a Condition of*   6
     Supernatural Revelation ... ...

§ IV. *The Possibility of a Revelation from the Philosophical Viewpoint*   8

§ V.   *The Interdependence of Revelation and Philosophy in Theology*   10

PART ONE.   **HE WHO IS**   13

   Chapter I. **God exists**   15

§ I.   *The Existence of God Is Not Self-Evident*   15

   I. The Teaching of Faith   15
     1. Sacred Scripture   15
     2. The teaching of the Fathers   16
     3. The doctrine of the Church   17

   II. The Understanding of Faith   18
     1. The idea of God does not imply an affirmation of his exis-
       tence   19
     2. The affirmation of being does not immediately imply the
       notion of divinity   20

Conclusion   21

§ II.   *The Existence of God Is Demonstrable*   22

I. The Teaching of Faith   22
  1. Sacred Scripture   22
  2. The teaching of the Fathers   24
  3. The doctrine of the Church   25

II. The Understanding of Faith   27
  1. The nature of demonstration   27
  2. The point of departure for the demonstration   27

§ III.   *The Affirmation of God's Existence Is True*   30

I. The Teaching of Faith   30
  1. The name of Yahweh   31
  2. Hebrew thought   32
  3. The Gospel of John   33
  4. The teaching of the Fathers   33
  5. First Vatican Council   35

II. The Understanding of Faith   35
  I. *The world as existing*   36
    1. Transcendence of esse   36
    2. The universality of esse or the act of existing   ...   37
    3. The actuality of esse or the act of existing   37
  II. *The world as effect*   38
    1. Being, the foundation of all intelligibility   38
    2. The lack of being implied in the ontological distinc-
       tion   39
    3. The necessity of a cause as a requisite for intelligi-
       bility   39
  III. *The affirmation of God's existence*   40
  IV. *The different methods of demonstration*   41
    1. Beginning with motion   42
    2. Beginning with the notion of efficient cause   43
    3. Beginning with the notion of contingency   44
    4. Beginning with the different degrees of perfection   44
    5. Finality   44
  V. *The role of demonstration*   46
  VI. *Implicit knowledge of God*   47

Conclusion   49

Chapter II.   **The essence of God**   51

ART. I. GOD'S ESSENCE IN ITSELF   51

§ I.   *God Is Simple: He Is Holy and Perfect*   52
I. The Teaching of Faith   52
  1. Sacred Scripture   52

  2. The teaching of the Fathers 55
  3. The doctrine of the Church 56

II. The Understanding of Faith 57
  1. God is spirit 57
  2. God is his essence 58
  3. God is his existence 59
  4. Pantheism 61

§ II.   *God Is One*   64

I. The Teaching of Faith 64
  1. The Old Testament 64
  2. The New Testament 67
  3. The teaching of the Fathers 68

II. The Understanding of Faith 68
  1. The experience of unity 69
  2. The reason for unity 70
  3. Necessity for a unique cause 71
  4. Unity of God 72
  5. The meaning of monotheistic faith 73

§ III.   *God Is Immutable and Eternal* 73

I. The teaching of Faith 73
  1. Sacred Scripture 73
  2. The teaching of the Fathers 75

II. The Understanding of Faith 76
  1. Time 76
  2. Duration 77
  3. Eternity 78

ART. II. GOD'S RELATIONSHIP TO MAN : THE DIVINE NAMES 79

I. The Teaching of Faith 79
  1. Sacred Scripture 79
  2. The teaching of the Fathers and Doctors of the Church 80

II. The Understanding of Faith 81
  1. The dialectic of knowledge 81
  2. God is incomprehensible yet knowable 84
  3. God is known by analogous knowledge 85
  4. The importance of analogy for theology 88

PART TWO.   **HE WHO ACTS** 91

Introduction 93

Chapter I. **God knows**   95

I. The Teaching of Faith   95
   1. The Old Testament   95
   2. The New Testament   97
II. The Understanding of Faith   98
   1. The fact of knowledge   98
   2. The "reason" for knowing   100
   3. Subsistent thought, cause of our thought   101
   4. The perfections of divine thought 102
   5. The content of God's knowledge   102

Chapter II. **God wills**   105

§ I.   *God Exists in an Act of Will* 105
I. The Teaching of Faith   105
II. The Understanding of Faith 106
   1. Freedom in God   106
   2. The efficacy of divine action 106
   3. The goal of divine action 107

§ II. *God Is Love: He Is Infinitely Good*   108
I. The Teaching of Faith   108
   1. St. John's statement: God is love 108
   2. The preparation of the Old Testament 108
   3. New Testament Doctrine 109
II. The Understanding of Faith 113
   1. God is love 113
   2. Disinterestedness of the Creator   116
   3. Divine preferences   117

§ III. *God Is Provident*   118
I. The Teaching of Faith   118
II. The Understanding of Faith 119
   1. The problem   119
   2. The principle of the answer   119
   3. The act of Providence   120
   4. The ways of Providence   121
   5. Recognition of providential action 121
   6. Providence and redemption   123
   7. Providence and evil 124

§ IV. *God Predestines*   125
I. The Teaching of Faith   125
   1. Holy Scripture: St. Paul 129
   2. The teaching of the Fathers: St. Augustine 128
   3. The doctrine of the Church   129

II. The Understanding of Faith 132
    1. The problem 132
    2. Human freedom and its limits 132
    3. The act of predestination 134
    4. The rejection of those eventually damned 136
    5. Predestination and reprobation 137

CONCLUSION 139

Index of biblical references 143

Index of Councils and documents 145

Index of proper names 146

Analytical index 148

TABLE OF THESES

Thesis I 18

Ratio humana, sine lumine gloriæ, non potest videre Deum (de fide) ; nec cognoscere aperte et immediate quod Deus sit : erroneum est dicere quod esse, per se notum in omnibus, est divinum ; tuto tradi non potest quod, sine immediata Dei cognotione, habituali saltem et non distincta a lumine intellectuali, intellectur humanus nihil cognoscere possit.

Human reason cannot see God without the aid of the light of glory (of Faith); nor can it know the existence of God immediately and clearly. It is erroneous to say that being, which makes itself known in all things, is a divine being; it cannot be taught with certitude that in the absence of an immediate, at least habitual, knowledge of God, (a knowledge which would be identical with the intellectual light), the human intellect can know nothing.

Thesis II 26

Deus unus et verus, creator et Dominus noster, per ea quæ facta sunt, naturali lumine, certo cognosci potest (de fide definita) ; adeoque tamquam causam per effectus demonstrari potest (doctrina communis).

The one and true God, our creator and lord, can be known with certainty with the natural light of human reason by means of things that have been made (defined of faith); his existence can also be demonstrated as a cause from its effect (common doctrine).

Thesis III 35

Dicit Dominus : Ego sum qui sum.

The Lord said: I am who I am.

Thesis IV 57

Deus est omnino simplex atque re et essentia a mundo distinctur (de fide definita).

God is absolutely simple and really and essentially distinct from the world (defined of faith).

Thesis V 68

Unus est Deus Pater Domini nostri Jesu Christi et non est alius præter eum (de fide).

God the Father of Our Lord Jesus Christ is one, and there is none other than he (of faith).

Thesis VI 76

Solus Deus est incommutabilis et æternus (de fide).

God alone is immutable and eternal (of faith).

Thesis VII   81

Deus est incomprehensibilis et ineffabilis (de fide), sed tamen aliqua nomina significant eum veraciter sed deficienter (doctrina communis).

God is incomprehensible and ineffable (of faith), however certain names signify him as he truly is, although in a less perfect manner (common doctrine).

Thesis VIII   98

Deus vivus et verus est intellectu perfectus; novit se et omnia quæ creavit verbo suo (de fide).

God, living and true, is perfect in intellect. He knows himself and all that he has created by his word (of faith).

Thesis IX   105

Deus est voluntate perfectus et liberrimo consilio condidit creaturam.

God is perfect in will, and whatever he has created, he has done by an absolutely free act (of faith).

Thesis X 113

Deus charitas est : in hoc cognovimus charitatem Dei quoniam Pater misit Filium suum salvatorem mundi ut nos, renati in Filio, diligamus qui prior dilexit nos.

God is love. We have known the love of God in that God has sent his Son as Saviour of the world so that we ourselves, reborn in the Son, would be able to love him who has loved us first.

Thesis XI   119

Universa, quæ condidit Deus providentia sua tuetur atque gubernat, attingens a fine usque ad finem fortiter et disponens omnia suaviter. Omnia enim nuda sunt oculis ejus, ea etiam quæ libera creaturarum actione futura sunt (de fide, Vat. Conc. I, S. III cap. I, Denz 1784)

Furthermore, by his providence God watches over and governs all things that he made, reaching from end to end with might and disposing all things with gentleness. For "all things are naked and open to his eyes," even those things that are going to occur by the free action of creatures (of faith).

Thesis XII   131

Deus in misericordia sua, prædestinavit salvandos in Salvatore ad gratiam in gloriam; reprobavit alios, sed neminem prædestinavit ad culpam (de fide).

In his mercy, God has predestined to grace and glory in the Saviour those who must be saved. He has rejected the others, but he has not predestined anyone to sin (of faith).

LIST OF ABBREVIATIONS

1. *Dictionaries, collections and periodicals:*

Denz   H. Denzinger, *Enchiridion symbolorum, definitionum et declarationum de rebus fidei et morum*, Barcelona, Herder, 1951.

DTC   *Dictionnaire de Théologie catholique*, published under the direction of A. Vacant, Paris, 1909 ff.

NRTh   *Nouvelle revue théologique*, Tournai.

PG   J. P. Migne, *Patrologiae cursus completus*, Series graeca, Paris-Montrouge, 1857-1866, 161 vols.

PL   J. P. Migne, *Patrologiae cursus completus*, Series latina, Paris-Montrouge, 1844-1864, 221 vols.

REA   *Revue des études augustiniennes.*

RHR   *Revue d'histoire des religions.*

RSPT   *Revue des sciences philosophiques et théologiques.*

RT   *Revue thomiste*, Toulouse and Paris.

2. *Books of the Bible:*

THE OLD TESTAMENT

Gen	Genesis	*Wis*	Wisdom
Ex	Exodus	*Sir*	Sirach (Ecclesiasticus)
Lev	Leviticus	*Is*	Isaiah
Num	Numbers	*Jer*	Jeremiah
Deut	Deuteronomy	*Lam*	Lamentations
Josh	Joshua	*Bar*	Baruch
Judg	Judges	*Ezek*	Ezekiel
Ruth	Ruth	*Dan*	Daniel
1 Sam	1 Samuel	*Hos*	Hosea
2 Sam	2 Samuel	*Joel*	Joel
1 Kings	1 Kings	*Amos*	Amos
2 Kings	2 Kings	*Obad*	Obadiah
1 Chron	1 Chronicles	*Jon*	Jonah
2 Chron	2 Chronicles	*Mic*	Micah
Ezra	Ezra	*Nahum*	Nahum
Neh	Nehemiah	*Hab*	Habakkuk
Tob	Tobit	*Zeph*	Zephaniah
Jud	Judith	*Hag*	Haggai
Esther	Esther	*Zech*	Zechariah

Job	Job	*Mal*	Malachi
Ps	Psalms	*1 Mac*	1 Maccabees
Prov	Proverbs	*2 Mac*	2 Maccabees
Eccles	Ecclesiastes		
Song	Song of Solomon		

THE NEW TESTAMENT

Mt	Matthew	*1 Tim*	1 Timothy
Mk	Mark	*2 Tim*	2 Timothy
Lk	Luke	*Tit*	Titus
Jn	John	*Philem*	Philemon
Acts	Acts of the Apostles	*Heb*	Hebrews
Rom	Romans	*Jas*	James
1 Cor	1 Corinthians	*1 Pet*	1 Peter
2 Cor	2 Corinthians	*2 Pet*	2 Peter
Gal	Galatians	*1 Jn*	1 John
Eph	Ephesians	*2 Jn*	2 John
Phil	Philippians	*3 Jn*	3 John
Col	Colossians	*Jude*	Jude
1 Thess	1 Thessalonians	*Rev*	Revelation (Apocalypse)
2 Thess	2 Thessalonians		

GENERAL BIBLIOGRAPHY

Sacred Scripture:

F. Ceuppens, *Theologia biblica* (Rome, 1938).

W. Eichrodt, *Theology of the Old Testament*, tr. by J. A. Baker (Phila., Pa.: Westminster Press, 1961).

A. Gelin, *The Key Concepts of the Old Testament*, tr. by George Lamb (New York: Sheed, 1955).

P. Heinisch, *Theology of the Old Testament*, tr. by W. Heidt (Collegeville, Minn.: Liturgical Press, 1950).

P. van Imschoot, *Théologie de l'Ancien Testament* (Paris-Tournai, 1954); Eng. tr. *Theology of the Old Testament*, Vol. I: *God* (New York: Desclée, 1965).

E. Jacob, *Theology of the Old Testament*, tr. by A. W. Heathcote and P. J. Allcock (New York: Harper, 1958).

G. Kittel, *Theological Dictionary of the New Testament*, tr. and ed. by G. W. Bromiley, Vol. I A-G (Grand Rapids, Mich.: Eerdmans, 1964).

C. Larcher, " La révélation de Dieu dans l'Ancien Testament, " *Initiation théologique* II (Paris, 1952) pp. 12-29.

O. Procksch, *Theologie des Altens Testaments* (Gutersloh, 1950).

K. Rahner, *Theological Investigations* I, tr. with Intro. by C. Ernst (Baltimore, Md.: Helicon, 1961).

C. Tresmontant, *A Study of Hebrew Thought*, tr. by M. F. Gibson (New York: Desclée, 1960).

Fathers of the Church:

B. Altaner, *Patrologie* (Freiburg im B.: Herder, 1951).

X. Le Bachelet, " Dieu, sa nature d'après les pères, " *DTC* IV, 1023-1151.

F. Cayré, *Précis de Patrologie et d'Histoire de la théologie* (Paris-Tournai-Rome: Desclée, 1931).

G. L. Prestige, *God in Patristic Thought* (London: S. P. C. K., 1956).

J. Quasten, *Patrology*, 2 Vols. (Westminster, Md.: Newman, 1950-1953).

J. Tixeront, *History of Dogmas*, tr. by H. L. Brianceau (St. Louis, Mo.: B. Herder, 1910).

Patristic texts treating specifically about God:

St. Anselm, *Monologion, PL* 158, 141-224; *Proslogion, PL* 158, 223-42.

St. Athanasius, *Contra Gentes, PG* 25, 3-96; Eng. tr. St. Athanasius, *Select Works and Letters,* Vol. 4 of the Second Series of A Select Library of Nicene and Post Nicene Fathers of the Christian Church (New York: C. Scribner, 1903), pp. 1-30.

Athenagoras, *Legatio pro Christianis,* cap. 1-9, 14-22, *PG* 6, 889, 915-42; Eng. tr. by J. H. Crehan, *Embassy for the Christians; The resurrection of the dead* (Westminster, Md.: Newman, 1956) pp. 29-40; 44-59.

St. Augustine, *De Vera Religione, PL* 34, 121-72; *De Trinitate;* Eng. tr. by S. McKenna, *The Trinity* (Wash., D. C.: Catholic University of America Press, 1963).

St. Basil, *Adversus Eunomium,* I-III, *PG* 29, 494-774; *Epistolae* 230-36, *PG* 32, 881-86; Eng. tr. by Sr. Agnes Clare Way, *Letters* (Wash., D. C.: Catholic University of America Press, 1955) pp. 152-72.

Clement of Alexandria, *Protrepticus* I, 2-7, *PG* 8, 67-186; *Stromata,* II, 2-4, V-VI, *PG* 8, 933-51; 9, 9-402 (Eng. tr., *Stromata or Miscellanies,* ed. by A. Roberts and J. Donaldson in Vol. 2 of a series: The Ante-Nicene Fathers (New York: Scribner, 1926) pp. 348-51; 444-523); *Paedagogus,* I, 8-9, *PG* 8, 326-56; Eng. tr. by S.P. Wood, *Christ the Educator* (New York: Fathers of the Church, Inc., 1954) pp. 56-78.

St. Cyril of Jerusalem, *Catechesis,* IV, VI, VIII, IX, *PG* 33, 453 ff; Eng. tr. by E.H. Gifford, *Catechetical Lectures* in Vol. 7 of the Second Series of A Select Library of Nicene and Post Nicene Fathers of the Christian Church (New York: Christian Literature Co., 1894) pp. 19-28, 33-43, 48-50, 51-56.

St. Gregory Nazianzen, *Orationes,* 27-31, *PG* 26, 11-172 Eng. tr. by C.G. Browne & J.E. Swallow, *Select Orations of St. Gregory Nazianzen* in Vol. 7 of the Second Series of A Select Library of Nicene and Post Nicene Fathers of the Christian Church (New York: Christian Literature Co., 1894) pp. 284-328.

St. Gregory of Nyssa, *Contra Eunomium, PG* 45, 243-1122; Eng. tr. by W. Moore & H.A. Wilson, *Against Eunomius* in Vol. 5 of the Second Series of A Select Library of Nicene and Post Nicene Fathers of the Christian Church (New York: Christian Literature Co., 1893) pp. 33-249.

St. Hilary of Poitiers, *De Trinitate,* I, *PG* 10, 25-49; Eng. tr. by S. McKenna, *The Trinity* (Wash., D.C.: Catholic University of America Press, 1954) pp. 3-34.

St. Irenaeus, *Adversus Haereses,* II, *PG* 7; Eng. tr. *Against the Heretics,* ed. by A. Roberts and J. Donaldson in Vol. 1 of a series: The Ante-Nicene Fathers (New York: Scribner, 1926) pp. 359-413.

St. John Chrysostom, *De Incomprehensibilitate Dei, PG* 48, 701-812.

St. John of Damascus, *De fide orthodoxa,* cap. 1-44, *PG* 94, 789 ff.; Eng. tr. by F.H. Chase, Jr., *Writings* (Wash., D. C.: Catholic University of America Press, 1958) pp. 165-266.

St. Justine, *Apologia*, I, 5-14, *PG* 6, 335-50; Eng. tr. by T.B. Falls, *Writings of St. Justine the Martyr* (New York: Christian Heritage, 1948) pp. 37-47.

Lactantius, *Divinae Institutiones*, I-IV, *PL* 6, 111-544 Eng. tr. by Sr. Mary Francis McDonald, *The Divine Institutes* (Wash., D.C.: Catholic University of America Press, 1964) pp. 15-325.

" Letter to Diognetum, " *(Epistola ad Diognetum) PG* 2, 1167-74, cc. 2-4; Eng. tr. by G.G. Walsh in *The Apostolic Fathers* (Wash., D.C.: Catholic University of America Press, 1947) pp. 355-58.

Minucius Felix, *Octavius*, 14-38, *PL* 275-357; Eng. tr. by R. Arbesmann, *Tertullian: Apologetical Works and Minucius Felix Octavius* (Wash., D.C.: Catholic University of America Press, 1950) pp. 344-401.

Novatian, *De Trinitate*, c. 1-10, *PL* 886-903; Eng. tr. ed. by A. Roberts and J. Donaldson in Vol. 5 of a series: The Ante-Nicene Fathers (New York: Scribner, 1926) pp. 611-20.

Origen, *Peri-Archon*, Prol. I, *PG* 11, 111-30; Eng. tr. ed. by A. Roberts and J. Donaldson in Vol. 4 of a series: The Ante-Nicene Fathers (New York: Scribner, 1926) pp. 237-67.

Pseudo-Denis, *De divinis nominibus*, *PL* 3, 585-996.

Tertullian, *Apologeticus*, 10-28, *PL* 1, 327-81; Eng. tr. ed. by A. Roberts and J. Donaldson in Vol. 3 of a series: The Ante-Nicene Fathers (New York: Scribner, 1926) pp. 26-41; *Adversus Marcionem*, I-II, *PL* 2, 239-320; Eng. tr. as above, pp. 271-320.

St. Theophilus of Antioch, *Ad Autolycum*, I; Eng. tr. ed. by A. Roberts and J. Donaldson in Vol. 2 of a series: The Ante-Nicene Fathers (New York: Scribner, 1926) pp. 89-93.

Declarations of the Church:

Hefele-Leclercq, *Histoire des Conciles* (Paris, 1907 ff).

J.M.A. Vacant, *Études théologiques sur les Constitutions du Concile du Vatican*, I, pp. 163-217; 271-329.

Theological speculation:

1. Mediaeval doctrine:

St. Anselm, *Monologion, PL* 158, 141-224; *Proslogion, PL* 158, 223-42.

St. Bonaventure, *Comm. in I Sent.* (Quaracchi, I); *The Works of Bonaventure*, tr. by José de Vinck, I, *Mystical Opuscula* (Paterson, N.J.: St. Anthony Guild Press, 1960), " The Journey of the Mind to God, " pp. 1-58.

M. Chossat, " Dieu, sa nature d'après les scolastiques, " *DTC* IV, cols. 1152-1243.

E. Gilson, *The Spirit of Mediaeval Philosophy*, tr. by A.H.C. Downes (New York: Scribner, 1936); *History of Christian Philosophy in the*

Middle Ages (New York: Random, 1955); *The Christian Philosophy of St. Thomas Aquinas*, tr. by L.K. Shook from the 5th edition (New York: Random, 1956); *The Philosophy of St. Bonaventure*, tr. by Dom Illtyd Trethowan and F.J. Sheed (London; Sheed, 1940); *Elements of Christian Philosophy* (Garden City, N.Y.: Doubleday, 1960); *John Duns Scot* (Paris: 1952).

P. Lombard, *Sententiae*, *PL* 191.

St. Thomas Aquinas, *Comm. in I Sent.* (Paris, 1929), Mandonnet ed.; *Truth*, 3 Vols. tr. by J.V. McGlynn, S.J. (Chicago: Regnery, 1953); *De Potentia* (Marietti: 1949); *On the truth of the Catholic Faith*, 4 Vols. tr. by Anton C. Pegis (Garden City, N.Y.: 1955); *Summa Theologica*. First complete American edition in 3 Vols. Literally translated by the Fathers of the English Dominican Province (New York: Benziger, 1947).

P. Vignaux, *Philosophy in the Middle Ages, An Introduction*, tr. by E.C. Hall (New York: Meridian, 1959).

M. de Wulf, *History of Mediaeval Philosophy*, 2 Vols. tr. by E.C. Messenger (New York: Dover, 1952).

2. Commentators and manuals:

Banez, *Comm. in I P. S. Thomae* (Duace, 1614).

B. Bartmann, *Précis de Théologie Dogmatique* (Mulhouse, 1947).

L. Billot, *De Deo Uno* (Rome, 1926).

Billuart, *Summa S. Thomae*, t. I-II.

Cajetan, *In Summ. Theol. Comm.* (Rome, ed. Leon.).

M. Daffara, *De Deo Uno* (Marietti, 1945).

S. de Ferrara, *In Summ. Contra Gentiles comm.* (Rome, ed. Leon.).

J.B. Franzelin, *Tractatus de Deo Uno* (Rome, 1910).

R. Garrigou-Lagrange, *De Deo Uno* (Rome, 1938).

John of St. Thomas, *In I P. Div. Thomae* (Paris-Tournai-Rome, 1931).

H. Paissac, "Dieu est," in *Initiation Théologique*, II (Paris, 1952), 33-142.

P. Parente, *De Deo Uno* (Rome, 1938).

D. Petavius, *Dogmata theologica de Deo Deique Proprietatibus*, t. I-II (Paris, 1865).

M. Scheeben, *Dogmatik*, v. 2 (Freiburg im B., 1873).

F. Suarez, *De Deo Uno* (Paris, 1861); *In Met. Arist. Disp.*, t. XXIX-XXX, XXVI (Paris, 1861).

A. Tanquerey, *Synopsis Theologiae Dogmaticae*, II (Paris, 1926).

L. Thomassinus, *Dogmata theologica*, t. I-II (Paris, 1864).

3. Modern studies:

U. von Balthasar, *Science, Religion and Christianity*, tr. by Hilda Graef (London: Burns, 1958).

R. Chauvin, *Dieu des savants, Dieu de l'expérience* (Mame).

J. Delanglade, *Le Problème de Dieu* (Paris: Aubier, 1960).

H. Duméry, *Le problème de Dieu en philosophie de la religion* (Desclée de Brouwer, 1957).

R. Guardini, *Le Dieu vivant* (Paris: Alsatia, 1956); Eng. tr. *The Living God*, by S. Godman (New York: Pantheon, 1957).

C. V. Héris, *Le Mystère de Dieu* (Paris: Siloé, 1946).

R. Jolivet, *The God of Reason*, tr. by Mark Pontifex (New York: Hawthorn, 1958).

C. Journet, *The Dark Knowledge of God*, tr. by J. F. Anderson (London: Sheed, 1948).

H. de Lubac, *The Discovery of God*, tr. by A. Dru (New York: Kenedy, 1960).

J. Maritain, *Approaches to God*, tr. by P. O'Reilly (New York: Harper, 1954).

J. H. Nicolas, *Connaître Dieu* (Paris: Cerf, 1947).

Périnelle, *Dieu est amour* (Paris: Cerf).

E. le Roy, *Introduction à l'étude du problème religieux* (Paris: Aubier 1944).

M. F. Sciacca, *L'existence de Dieu* (Paris: Aubier, 1951).

A. D. Sertillanges, *Les sources de la croyance en Dieu* (Paris: Perrin, 1931); *Catéchisme des incroyants* (Paris: Flammarion, 1931); *Dieu ou rien* (Paris: Flammarion, 1931); *Foundations of Thomistic Philosophy*, tr. by G. Anstruther (New York: Herder, 1931).

F. van Steenberghen, *Dieu caché* (Louvain: Nauwelaerts, 1911).

E. Suhard, " The Meaning of God, " reprint of the Eng. tr. of a pastoral letter issued by the Archbishop of Paris at Eastertime, 1948, in *Integrity* III (Feb., 1949) no. 5.

C. Tresmontant, *Essai sur la connaissance de Dieu* (Paris: Cerf, 1959); Eng. tr. by R. J. Olsen, *Toward the Knowledge of God* (Baltimore: Helicon, 1961).

De la connaissance de Dieu (Ouvrage collectif), *Recherches de Philosophie III-IV* (Desclée de Brouwer, 1958).

L'existence de Dieu (Ouvrage collectif) (Casterman, 1962).

4. The relationship of theology with philosophy:

E. Borne, *Atheism*, tr. by S. J. Tester (New York: Hawthorn, 1961).

E. Gilson, *God and Philosophy* (New Haven, Conn.: Yale University Press, 1941).

R. Jolivet, *Études sur le problème de Dieu dans la pensée contemporaine* (Lyon-Paris: Vitte, 1932).

J. Lacroix, *La signification de l'athéisme contemporain* (Paris: Aubier, 1950).

H. de Lubac, *Le drame de l'humanisme athée* (Paris: Spes, 1944).

M. F. Sciacca, *L'existence de Dieu* (Paris: Aubier, 1951); *Le problème de Dieu dans la philosophie contemporaine* (Paris: Aubier, 1950).

§ I Theology and Theodicy

Since the legitimacy of a theology of the One God has been occasionally contested, one wonders whether such a theology is at all conceivable. To make an abstraction out of the mystery of the Trinity is apparently to regress to the views of a philosopher. As a result, every properly theological characteristic of St. Thomas' *De Deo Uno* would have to be denied. Yet without discounting the value of such an effort on the strictly rational level it is quite difficult to find a place between biblical theology and philosophical theodicies for a theology truly worthy of that name, i.e. one careful to draw its object from no source other than revelation, but equally careful to understand this object with the aid of arguments prepared by philosophy. In a word, it is difficult to imagine any possible point of contact at all between the God of Jesus Christ and the God of the philosophers.

1. *Faith, the source of theology*

This, however, would not be so much a reduction of theology to a simple explanation of the faith, as a denial of its proper nature. True, theology begins by listening to faith, i.e. by humbly submitting to revelation, but it develops only in the understanding of faith, which is the work of reason. And how else could this understanding be acquired except that rational reflection be put at the disposal of faith? This is what St. Thomas did in his *Summa Theologica*. The theology of God, however, in spite of its rational appearance, is no less radically different from philosophical theodicies.

This is true from a threefold point of view. Firstly, theology by its *intention* surpasses by far the goal which philosophy sets for itself. The philosopher speaks of God only because he is forced to do so to guarantee and ground the problematic existence of the things of this world. " God " is not the subject of his science. On the other hand, the theologian speaks of God in order to understand what God has said about himself.   The God of philosophy comes as an answer to the question posed by the world's existence.   But the God of faith reveals his existence only in order to enter into direct and personal communion with the believer.

Secondly, theology also differs from theodicy by its *content*.   True, it does overlap the domain of philosophy to a large extent.   Yet philosophy does nothing else but affirm the existence of a primary intelligent and free cause.   The God of the theologian is entirely different.   He spoke through his prophets, became incarnate in Jesus Christ, and provided for men a destiny which no philosopher could even imagine. [1]   Even though theology at the outset does not consider the mystery of the Trinity, it never loses sight of it.   Moreover, theology considers questions totally unforeseeable by philosophy, questions posed only by faith, e.g. predestination, the vision of God, and providence.

Finally, insofar as theology stems from faith and remains under the control of the Magisterium, it participates in a *certitude* which has never been the lot of philosophical doctrines.

Yet even while conceding that the object of theology surpasses that of theodicy, it could still be objected that on certain points, e.g. the existence of God, theology is hardly distinguishable from philosophy. [2] Is there any difference between the demonstration of the theologian and that of the philosopher?   None at all, if we consider the structure of the proof; all the difference in the world, if we consider the intention which guides it.   The experience of a world which is not self-sufficient inspires the philosopher's reflection.   Revelation furnishes the truth with which the theologian begins.   The theologian seeks to understand what he believes.   God said to Moses: " I am. "   What is the meaning of " I am? "   That is the question asked in theology.   But no philosopher has posed the problem in this manner.   The fact that the explanation of faith proposed in theology attains under these circumstances to the rigor of a demonstration does not change a thing.   This demonstration is not sought as an end in itself.   It *follows* upon faith and does not precede it.   The demonstration might not work out at all.   Even if he has to be content with probable arguments, or mere reasons of convenience, as is often the case in other realms of theology, the theologian will not be disturbed at all.   The certitude of the truth which he explains derives from a different source.

---

[1] A. R. Motte, " Théodicée et théologie chez saint Thomas d'Aquin, " *RSPT* 26 (1953) 5-26.
[2] Cf. the excellent remarks of E. Gilson, *Elements of Christian Philosophy* (Garden City, N. Y.: Doubleday & Co., Inc., 1960) pp. 22-42.

2. *Faith and demonstration*

It could be insisted, and rightly so, that faith is incompatible with a truth acquired by demonstration. There is common agreement that the theologian makes faith his point of departure; in this sense his explanation fulfills an intention different from that of the philosopher. But if the explanation gives place to a successful demonstration, the evidence of reason supplants faith on the demonstrated point; thus through an action of theology, the believer becomes a philosopher. For St. Thomas, one and the same truth could not be simultaneously and under the same aspect an object of both faith and science. In point of fact, science entails evidence, or a possible deduction from evidence, so that the object of science demands the mind's adherence on the force of a mediate or immediate demonstration. In faith, on the other hand, a demonstration is totally lacking. The mind adheres to a proposed truth on the force of a motive extrinsic to this truth, namely, trust in the veracity of an eye-witness. Under these conditions, it is clear that faith and science are mutually exclusive, since one and the same truth could not at one and the same time and under the same aspect be evident and not-evident. And yet as a matter of fact God's existence is revealed to those who are unable to prove it. In this case, however, the revealed truth is not supernatural in substance, since it is demonstrable. I cannot believe by an act of supernatural faith that God is the first cause of the world, if I also accept this as true because of a demonstration from natural reason alone.

In order to allay certain fears, however, let us note that the theologian who elaborates this demonstration in no way loses the merit of his faith, provided that he approach this task, not as a preliminary step to his belief, but for the purpose of acquiring an understanding of his faith and out of obedience to this same faith which assures us that a proof for the existence of God is possible. In thus offering to God the homage of his reason, the theologian does not destroy his faith; rather he leads it to its perfection.

3. *Faith, knowledge of salvation*

Nevertheless, it is true that the theologian by no means is dispensed from believing that God exists. The obligation imposes itself even upon him each time his salvation comes into question, i.e. every time that he has to stake his life on an indubitable certitude. As rigorous and certain as it might be, scientific demonstration actually proceeds from a naturally fallible reason. An error can always slip into the course of reasoning. The certitude of faith on the other hand enjoys the

infallibility of the very word of God (*STh*, II-II, a. 4, q. 8).   True, faith
is more obscure and demonstration surpasses it in *clarity* (II-II, a. 4, q. 8,
ad 3), but faith is more *firm* and its adherence more strong, since it rests
on the revelation of him who is Truth itself.   Here the motive of adherence
—the word of God—overturns our natural hierarchy.   Ordinarily the
degree of certitude grows in proportion to the degree of evidence, but
the absolutely irrefutable character of the certitude of faith derives
not from the evidence of its object, but from the quality of the witness,
who is God, the immediate source of certitude.   If now one seeks the
"reasons" for this supplementary certitude which God grants by
revelation, it immediately becomes clear that this revelation would
hardly have any meaning at all if it would establish nothing more than the
natural truth of the existence of God.   As a matter of fact, however, God
does reveal his existence, but only in order to call man to the vision
of his essence and thereby to share in his happiness.   Thus in the measure
to which the affirmation that God exists is implied in the structure of
truths believed with supernatural faith, belief in the existence of God
imposes itself upon every man.   The philosopher thus can demonstrate
the existence of the world's first cause, and the theologian who borrows
his demonstration will accept the conclusion on evidence from the rational
order; in this sense he no longer believes.   But insofar as this conclusion
is linked to the affirmation of a Saviour-God who has manifested himself
in Jesus Christ, it is believed on faith, because this truth is not known
by reason under this particular aspect.   The existence of God, then, is the
object of faith insofar as this knowledge directs a man to happiness.
Consequently, no matter how one considers the problem, theology can
never be confused with theodicy.   The basic reason is that theology
considers God as he manifests himself in the Faith.   Yet it is no less
true that the philosopher also speaks of God.   Theology therefore of
necessity poses the question of the relationships between faith and
reason.

§ II.   Natural and Supernatural Manifestation of God

God manifests himself to men in the various expressions of his word.
For the believer, the fact that God speaks is an event proven by all
creation, since everything that exists, including the internal certitude of
faith, is sustained by his word.   In point of fact, God manifests himself
in many ways which are the results of the different effects of his creative
word.   Everything speaks of God, but in a different way.   Let us

distinguish, among many possibilities, two kinds of word: that which *builds*, so to speak, by which God created heaven and earth and all they contain; and that which *speaks*, purely and simply, by which God can say: " I, " and reveal himself. These two types of word both manifest the unique creative word, but they are quite distinct by virtue of their effect. One is creative of truth, the other creative of reality. They do not manifest God in the same way.

When God speaks in order to make *something*, the object or effect of his word is not to say, " God. " Certainly the created object is not totally mute, since it does manifest God as its creator, but it " shows " more than it " says. " In order to speak of God, the object must recede to the background, for in itself it is not God. The object manifests him only by subtle allusion; in fact, the object itself is this allusion. That is why God's manifestation which is given in the created object on man's part requires an interpretation, which he and he alone makes.

On the other hand, when God speaks in order to produce a *word* which reveals him, he himself coincides with the very object of this word. While the created object must cause itself to be forgotten to speak of God, the revealed word expresses God by the very fact that it exists as word. It came from God and returns to him, remaining all the while entirely unchanged. Thus the manifestation of God which is accomplished in an extrinsic manner in the creative word, is realized in an interior and essential manner in the revealing word. No human interpretation could add to its content. It suffices for man to listen in order to know and understand how to welcome, in the spirit of obedience, a revelation which, precisely because it is supernatural, does not come from within man himself.

Supernatural revelation, however, does not suppress the necessity of a natural manifestation of God—especially since it surpasses the latter in extension and comprehension. Rather all the more it implies a natural manifestation. First of all, the revealed word, such as the Magisterium of the Church has defined it, teaches the possibility of a natural knowledge of God, the source and goal of the universe. This possibility lies within the pale of revelation. On the other hand, the human word in the degree to which it goes beyond the order of action and approaches the expression of THAT WHICH EXISTS absolutely, in the ultimate analysis becomes a word about God; he who is. This means that the language of being can serve as a means of communication between God who reveals himself and his human spokesman. In fact, language defines the field of possible revelation. If there is a divine meaning of being, philosophy at its summit changes into theology. And this means that the affirmation of the existence of God is located at the meeting point between revelation and philosophy.

This is indeed a delicate encounter, in which philosophy and theology which derives from revelation risk a mutual compromise. If metaphysics is *knowledge* through and through, how could it dare to invade the pale of faith even on one point? On the other hand, if revelation is *the ultimate truth* about that which exists, how could it leave the question of authenticity to metaphysics? It is true that faith, relying on revelation, considers God as the basic and primary meaning of the act of existence, in a knowledge in which the answer gratuitously precedes each question. Thus the very first question contests metaphysics and the philosopher is correct in saying that " philosophy dies in contact with the absolute "; or that metaphysics, as knowledge of being, becomes, in the long run, a knowledge of divine being. Revelation then loses its object and the theologian is correct in seeing in natural theology " an attack on the Christian idea of God. " [3]

A deeper examination of the problem, however, shows that revelation and philosophy are not at all mutually exclusive, provided that the two following points are kept in mind: that philosophy be lived through and through as a perpetual *question;* and that faith truly be a harkening to a supernatural *revelation* from God about God.

§ III.   The Possibility of a Natural Knowledge of God as a Condition of Supernatural Revelation

Revelation not only asserts the possibility of a natural knowledge of God, but it rightfully requires this natural knowledge as a *conditio sine qua non.* The harm resulting from a radical denial of a natural knowledge of God is that it destroys the very possibility of a revelation. The idea of revelation unquestionably implies, on the one hand, that it be conceived as the removal of a secret. Hence it must be the effect of God's free initiative (in the absence of which there would be no revelation). On the other hand, the notion also implies that it represent for man, to whom it is addressed, a free and gratuitous gift (otherwise revelation would not be supernatural). Now how could man recognize the initiative of a free gift in revelation, if he doesn't even know of the existence of a God, who alone decides whether to speak or keep silent? The supernatural character of revelation logically cannot be understood except in reference to a natural knowledge of God. This latter fact is a must if man is supposed

---

[3] L. Malevez, " Le croyant et le philosophe, " *NRTH* 82 (1960) pp. 897-917.

to be capable of recognizing revelation as a gracious gift from God. "...For in the nature of things he (man) has also to reckon with God's silence. In other words, even naturally speaking man must stand before God conceived of as a free Person transcending the world. " [4]

Furthermore, in the absence of even the possibility of a natural knowledge of God, not only would the *fact* of a divine word become improbable, but the very *content* of revelation would be *a priori* devoid of substance, since this content is not self-evident. By the very fact that revelation expresses in human words the mystery of God, it involves a constant reference to the realities of our universe. The mystery is precisely that these realities go so far as to signify a personal Principle transcending the universe. Consequently, if this personal principle is listed among the unknowable, revelation no longer has an object. What good is it then to know that there is a Father, Son, and a Holy Spirit, if one loses sight of the fact that these Three Persons constitute one and the same God? What meaning can be given to the word " God, " if one cannot conceive him philosophically as the supreme Existent, creator of heaven and earth? The " Christian God " cannot cease being the "principle God " of the world toward whom human reflection is directed. Otherwise, the mystery would disappear; there would be no revelation *about God*. Likewise, the God of Abraham in no way can be other than the God-Author of the universe. The revealed mystery bears precisely upon the identity of the Three Persons with Him-Who-Is. [5]

In order to hear revelation it is not necessary that the human subject must have an explicit knowledge of the proofs for God's existence. But it is indispensable that he have the power to do so. This potentiality is nothing more than an openness of mind to an eventual revelation in the absence of which not only would revelation be objectively unrealizable, but man would be unable to take a stand, i.e. to accept (or reject) the Word of God. Freedom in acceptance obviously demands an *aptitude* on the subject's part to receive revelation. God does not manifest himself to the pebbles along the roadside. He addresses only a subject capable of understanding. This presupposes a natural, internal capacity in man that prepares him to receive grace. Undoubtedly this interior disposition in the subject did not come into existence independently of creative action,

[4] K. Rahner, *Theological Investigations* I, tr. by Cornelius Ernst (Baltimore, Md.: Helicon Press, 1961) p. 84.

[5] H. Bouillard, *Karl Barth* III, p. 102: " Except for a natural knowledge of God (implicit though it be) we would have no principle of judgment which would allow us to truly establish our recognition of a divine revelation in history; nothing would allow us to affirm that the God of the Bible is our God also. "

but it is not to be identified with revelation. In this regard revelation does not create its own subject; revelation is only an event experienced by a subject who already has his own resources. In the realm of effects, one must distinguish between the acts by which God gives existence to a spirit, and the act by which he reveals himself. This points to the fact that the subject exists prior to revelation and is not brought into existence by it. Thus it is in virtue of a natural power that " man is capable of opening himself to God who encounters him and reveals himself to him. " The actuation of this potentiality, as it is effected in knowledge based on faith, beyond all shadow of a doubt surpasses man's forces. Yet for man to perceive this it is necessary that he be capable of measuring it in relationship to the ultimate development of his knowledge; moreover, that this latter knowledge must allow him to view himself, on this side of revelation, as the subject of a possible revelation, because of power which is connatural to him. This power thus would include the possibility of a natural knowledge of God. Such a possibility would appear to be a *sine qua non* condition for a supernatural revelation.

§ IV. The Possibility of a Revelation from the Philosophical Viewpoint

Philosophically it is impossible to prove the necessity of revelation. But one can deduce its possibility by beginning from philosophical reflection and showing that the rational denial of such an eventuality would undermine philosophy itself.

The characteristic quality of philosophy is that it should " awaken us to the problems of the existence of the world and our own existence. " The question of being is not an ordinary question. The astonishment which the existence of this world causes forces us to descend to the root of all astonishment. Every question presupposes the question of being. This means that the quest for being underlies the fundamental project of knowledge. But it must be added that the accomplishment of this project must remain ever in abeyance. This is the paradox of the question of being: being is at one and the same time the term under discussion and the light of every possible answer. We can conclude from this fact that strictly speaking " one cannot investigate being; one can only raise questions by beginning with being. " [6]

---

[6] G. Marcel, " L'être devant la pensée interrogative, " *Bull. Soc. fr. de Ph.* 52 (1958) 9.

Since being poses the question, it is a question without an answer, without a human answer. The question is too basic to be solved by a theoretical explanation. In fact in regard to problems of interest to us, we can investigate only incidentally by means of the existents of this world, viz., a domain in which the mind is master of its problems and their answers. Every true and enlightening solution to the problems raised by the presence of being is not to be excluded. Every answer given to *definite problems* must be placed within the context of the question of being— a question conceived as a search. No reply of the philosophical order can put a definitive end to the investigation of being.

At this time we must distinguish between *problem* and *investigation*. Philosophy has for its object putting an end to all problems. The apparent contradictions which the apparitions of being raises on the level of immediate experience create a problem. Philosophy arrives at an answer which can be considered as certain by telling what the presence of being is not, by separating being from its diverse and contingent manifestations. In the long run this answer boils down to an affirmation of the existence of subsisting being. It matters little that this or that philosophy in point of fact contests this answer. In the eyes of the theologian it has some possibility. The philosopher cannot reproach him for *ignoring* the basic nature of the question of being, because he doesn't.

By his own efforts man will never succeed definitively in illuminating the shadows surrounding this question. The affirmation of subsisting being is no exception. In order to reach definitive enlightenment, one must eliminate all mediation. The statement of the problem, however, presupposes a mediation between man and God. More profoundly, the fact of the question presupposes in man a finitude which he cannot transcend. The entire metaphysical effort (problem and solution) is worked out within the context of a question which never ceases to exist. This only shows that the object of metaphysics, at the limits of metaphysics, continues to remain the object of desire, of investigation, but it is an investigation, however, devoid of all difficulties. " The last step of reason is to recognize that there is an infinity of things which surpass it. "

It is evident that the affirmation of God's existence (no matter if it comes from reason or faith) resolves certain problems, but does not do away with the statement of the question, because the question infinitely surpasses the problems to be resolved. Theology has been reproached for using metaphysical astonishment only to motivate a statement which puts an end to the astonishment. Nothing could be further from the truth! Primitive astonishment, which being awakens, strengthens the

affirmation of subsistent being. But in no way does the affirmation of
God's existence fix a limit to metaphysical inquiry. This inquiry rather
focuses upon the source of every question. In precise fashion it delineates
the dark areas of the mind and its essential " night. " In fact, it is God's
mysterious presence that gives the metaphysical inquiry its bearing and
universal scope. " The companion of the philosopher, the stranger, the
invisible guest of metaphysics " is not " nothing, " as Heidegger would
wish; it is pure being, it is God.

Thus at the limits of metaphysics one discovers the possibility of a
revelation. Since being is the ultimate object of thought and always
remains fundamentally under investigation, metaphysics remains an open
science. It is knowledge of the absolute, but not absolute knowledge.
The answers it provides undoubtedly give some satisfaction in that which
concerns contingent beings. That which concerns being itself still remains
the object of investigation. A revelation from being about being is
therefore not impossible. This essential revelation is most certainly due
only to the free initiative of being. By its very content, which is the
intimacy of Him Who Is, it engenders in this man a knowledge which by
its nature surpasses all natural knowledge. Being reveals itself therein,
not as the ultimate intelligible object in this world, but insofar as it
surpasses reason. Natural reason affirms that God is the cause of the
world because he is He Who Is. Only he who has said, " I am who am, "
can take the revelation to its term: " I am he who is the Father, Son, and
Holy Spirit. "

§ V.   The Interdependence of Revelation and Philosophy in Theology

Although revelation surpasses philosophy in depth, it does not destroy
it or absorb it. It is true that both of them develop a certain knowledge
of God, but they are not identical in their object or in their method.
Metaphysics seeks an understanding of being insofar as it appears in a
problematic manner in the world; in passing through the world, it seeks all
evidence which does not contradict being. In the final analysis this is its
title to the term, " knowledge of God. " On the other hand, faith
recognizes God *immediately*, but it does not *know*. It is a recognition of
those things which are not seen. What we learn by faith, we adhere to by
the testimony of Christ, who himself has seen. He speaks to us, however,
in words which do not allow us to see. The essential domain of faith does
not reveal those things in which being is manifest in the world: that is the
domain of philosophy. Faith rather recounts that aspect in which Being

is radically hidden in the world, i.e. the domain of its intimacy. Faith therefore is living in being insofar as Being is Night; and this Night cannot be dissipated by any human word, even that of faith. The knowledge which Faith gives, although true, positive and certain, is essentially enclosed in that Night of Being. This is what leaves to philosophy all its freedom; faith which is hidden in this Night does not cramp philosophy, nor is it itself cramped by philosophy.

The independence of faith and philosophy should not cause us to forget the reciprocal action that they exercise upon one another. Of itself, philosophy is independent of faith; it can arise and exist without it. But from the historical point of view it is clear that it cannot be disinterested in revelation. Revelation keeps philosophy in its investigations and maintains it in its prologue. One can no longer say of the philosopher who by rationalism would reject the God of Abraham in order to safeguard the God of reason, that he has true knowledge of God, [7] because he would deny the possibility of this God ever revealing himself. Conversely, although in its origin faith is independent of philosophy it cannot continue to exist without rational support; and if the reasoning process is carried out with diligence and precision it will unavoidably encounter the pre-existent philosophy underlying the very truths of faith.

Just as grace presupposes nature, faith, or more specifically theology which includes faith, presupposes at least an implicit natural knowledge of God, which serves as a preamble and as a subject of the propositions of faith. [8] In the absence of this metaphysical introduction, revelation could not be understood. Man's metaphysical vocation makes revelation a possibility and maintains it in its supernatural character. One should not therefore be astonished if the Church, interpreting revelation to conserve it in its purity, has given decisions which theologians must take into account regarding the possibility and nature of the natural knowledge of God.

[7] *STh* II-II, q. 10, a. 3.
[8] *Ibid.*, I, q. 2, a. 2, ad 1.

PART ONE

HE WHO IS

CHAPTER ONE

GOD EXISTS

§ I. The Existence of God Is Not Self-Evident

I. THE TEACHING OF FAITH

The human mind is impelled by a natural propensity to seek evidence in all things. Moreover, the impact of evidence increases as it emerges with greater clarity into the open. Therefore in the presence of him who is clarity personified, illuminating everything about him, how could the mind fail to see the evidence? Isn't God evident?

It is important to be careful not to confuse two basic problems: that of the evidence of God's existence, and that of seeing God in his intimate mystery.

1. *Sacred Scripture*

In regard to the second problem, Sacred Scripture has an unequivocal answer: God is invisible. True, he did appear under a visible form in many Old Testament narratives. He walked in the garden in the cool of the evening; Adam saw him. Then Abraham saw him from the entrance to his tent (Gen 18). Jacob fought with him hand to hand (Gen 25). Moses spoke with him face to face (Ex 33). In a more ethereal vision Micaiah and Isaiah saw him seated upon his throne, surrounded by the heavenly host (1 Kgs 22,19; Is 6), etc. But these anthropomorphisms are quite clear and not at all deceptive. This God, so human and so near, nevertheless remains a hidden God. Moses saw him only from behind and Isaiah spied naught else but his coat-tails. Still, Israel progressed in the course of its history to an increasingly rigorous purification of its faith. Allusions to contacts that are too base begin to be avoided. Intermediaries between God and his spokesmen begin to multiply. Visions diminish in meaning to the point of being less visions of reality than symbolic events. In fact they are restricted to one fundamental purpose in the religion of Israel: the revelation of the word.

It has been observed that theophanies never took place as ends in themselves—in order to be contemplated—but rather for the transmission of a message. If God manifests himself, it is only in order to speak. [1] It sometimes happens that the vision becomes suspect when it contradicts the content of the word. It is the truth of the word that governs criticism as well as interpretation. The lasting element of this transitory vision is the word. " The *word* is a fullness of the *mind.* " [2] Revelation is definitively acquired only by an understanding of the word. But the knowledge which the word engenders is faith, in other words a knowledge which on principle excludes evidence. The New Testament sheds decisive details on this subject. " For we walk by faith, not by sight, " writes St. Paul (2 Cor 5,7). " (God) alone is immortal, his home is in inaccessible light, and no man has seen or is able to see him " (1 Tim 6,16). " No one has ever seen God, " concludes St. John (1 Jn 4,12). The vision of God is relegated to the next life.

In regard to the first point (the fáct of the existence of God), Scripture has no explicit answer. In the thought and behavior of the Hebrew people the existence of God was never questioned; it was not even doubted, except perhaps to make some other point. It would be the height of stupidity to say in one's heart " There is no God! " (Ps 53,2). Even so, this exclamation expresses only revolt, not denial. In their polemics against the pagans, the sacred authors could not even imagine that these men, deprived of revelation, could contest the existence of God: they took issue with pagan idolatry and the ignorance that it presupposed, rather than with their atheism. It is nevertheless remarkable that, in their refutation of pagan errors, the sacred authors made no appeal to an intuitive evidence of the existence of God, but were satisfied in suggesting reflection upon the works of creation. They did not even think of depending upon any evidence to which a simple reference would suffice (cf. Wis 13; Rom 1). This argument from silence must be kept in mind.

2. *The teaching of the Fathers*

The Fathers take up the teaching of Scripture and give it fuller explanation. In the measure to which they underscore God's incomprehensibility, the Fathers discard the possibility of a natural intuition of God. God is ineffable. No language can give adequate expression to him. That is what the Cappadocian Fathers hold, in opposition to Eunomius. God is invisible. He manifests himself, however, by his creative work

[1] F. Michaeli, *Dieu à l'image de l'homme* (Neuchâtel: Delachaux et Niestlé) p. 156.

[2] A. Neher, *L'essence du prophétisme* (Paris: PUF) p. 110.

and his providential actions. The power of the Invisible One makes the pre-eminence of his omnipotence visible, as St. Irenaeus would say in substance. An idea common to a good number of the Fathers is that the manifestation of God is in some way congenital with the human mind: it is a " seed of light, " a " seal imprinted " upon the mind. Summarizing the thought of his predecessors, St. John Damascene wrote: " For through nature the knowledge of the existence of God has been revealed by him to all men. " [3]

3. *The doctrine of the Church*

Little by little the Church clarified her doctrine. The Council of Paris in 1227, approved by the Pope, denounced the error of those who held to a " natural and immediate knowledge of the first Cause. " [4] In regard to the natural *vision* of God, it was unequivocally condemned by the ecumenical Council of Vienne in 1311 (Denz 475). In the 19th century, the Magisterium of the Church issued a series of warnings against ontologism as taught by Malebranche. In 1861 a decree of the Holy Office declared that the following proposition could not be taught with certitude: " An immediate knowledge of God, which is at least habitual, is so essential to the human intellect that without that knowledge it can know nothing. It is the light of the intellect itself " (Denz 1659). The entire proposition and its implications is suspect, although there is no question here of a formal condemnation. A similar disapproval was leveled at the theses which Branchereau, a theologian from Nantes, had submitted to Rome for judgment: " It does not suffice to distinguish *ens simpliciter* from *ens secundum quid* in order to know God. " [5] Much later at the First Vatican Council, certain Fathers called for the formal condemnation of ontologism. The Bishops of Naples and Perouse had proposed the following statement for condemnation: " The direct and immediate knowledge of God is natural to man, " but the Council disbanded before completing its work. It condemned nothing more than the form of ontologism included in pantheism. Finally, certain errors of Rosmini were denounced in 1887 by the Holy Office: it is erroneous to hold that the manifestation of indeterminate being in creatures can be identified with evidence of God, or divinity (Denz 1894).

---

[3] *De fide orthodoxa*, chaps. 1 and 3, *PG* 44, 789 and 793. English translation: St. John of Damascus, *Writings*, tr. by Fredric H. Chase, Jr. (Washington, D. C.: Catholic University of America Press, 1958) p. 166.

[4] *DTC*, " Ontologisme, " 1046.

[5] *Ibid.*, 1050.

Thesis I. *Ratio humana, sine lu-mine gloriæ, non potest videre Deum* (de fide); *nec cognoscere aperte et immediate quod Deus sit: erroneum est dicere quod esse, per se notum in omnibus, est divinum; tuto tradi non potest quod, sine imme-diata Dei cognitione, habituali sal-tem et non distincta a lumine intellectuali, intellectus humanus nihil cognoscere possit.*

Human reason cannot see God without the aid of the light of glory *(of Faith)*; nor can it know the existence of God immediately and clearly. It is erroneous to say that being, which makes itself known in all things, is a divine being; it cannot be taught with certitude that in the absence of an immediate, at least habitual, knowledge of God (a knowledge which would be identical with the intellectual light), the human intellect can know nothing.

II.   THE UNDERSTANDING OF FAITH

How is this proposition of faith to be understood: The existence of God is not an object of immediate evidence?

The question centers on evidence, and this word evokes the idea of clarity. What can be seen is evident. Silver is a seen metal. Not that silver itself can cause someone to see it; but it is bright enough to come into view; it is evident. And yet it must reflect some light in order to be seen. The sun on the other hand knows no such dependency; it is objectively self-evident.

But there can be no evidence without a seeing-subject. And this seeing-subject recognizes many degrees of evidence. The highest degree of evidence is an existential kind of evidence. When I see that day is breaking, my certitude is immediate. It suffices to open one's eyes to notice that it is day and not night. Still more clear and more intimate is the evidence I have when I think that I think, for in this case evidence is identical with the act of seeing. This is a case of immediate intuitive evidence.

Evidence of a lesser degree would be that on the representative order. This is the case when I conceive that Socrates is a man. The definition is evident, yet it is not strictly immediate. There no longer exists that kind of identity which is immediately perceived between the mind which thinks and the thought which is thought. In my *idea* of a man, the object seen is not identical with the one who sees. The abstract idea (man) intervenes as a medium. This is a case of mediate intuitive evidence.

1. *The idea of God does not imply an affirmation of his existence*

Similar precisions lead us to distinguish two questions in the problem of God's existence. To begin with: is the existence of God an evidence of the representative type? Does the idea of God imply the affirmation of his existence? The question is not as foolish as it might appear. It suffices to compare the idea of God to that which we can conceive of other existents in order to understand that we are faced with a unique case. When the idea of silver is presented to my mind, its content causes me to know the nature of silver, but it tells me nothing about the existence of silver outside of my mind. The existence of silver outside of the mind is not included in the reason of money (nor in the fact of its existence in the core of my mind). Considering only the reason for this thing, I do not see included therein the affirmation of its existence. In order to assure myself of this, I must appeal to evidence of a different order: viz., to sensible experience.

And yet it seems that the idea of God possesses a characteristic that legitimizes the tendency of many thinkers to unhesitatingly proclaim that his existence is evident. It is clear that in the proposition " God exists, " the predicate *exists* is contained immediately and necessarily in the subject *God*. How can one think of God without thinking of an existing being? If, following St. Anselm, by this word *God* we understand a being greater than which no other can be conceived, he must necessarily exist. It is greater to exist than not to exist, to exist outside of my mind than to exist only within my mind. Since supreme perfection belongs to God by definition, existence comes into clear evidence in the very meaning of his name.

How strong is this argument? Does the idea of God, conceived as unsurpassable, also include the idea of his existence? Yes, if I consider what happens in my mind, and this is precisely how this idea differs from every other idea. But as Gilson writes, " the idea of existence is never the equivalent of actual existence. "[6] If it were only a question of *notions*, the argument would be irreproachable. But the reasoning errs when it concludes to the *affirmation* of a God existing outside of the mind. It smooths over an equivocation on the word " existence, " which signifies both the content of a notion, and actual existence outside of my mind.

---

[6] E. Gilson, *The Christian Philosophy of St. Thomas Aquinas*, tr. by L. K. Shook (London: Victor Gollancz, Ltd., 1957) pp. 54-55.

Now nothing can force me to say that there actually exists some reality corresponding to my idea of an unsurpassable-existent-outside-of-the-mind. God cannot not-exist, certainly: it is presupposed that he is. If we presupposed that he did not exist there would remain only the idea of a God who could not-not-exist. Between the idea of a necessarily existing God and the affirmation of his existence outside of the mind there is a distance which reason sees but cannot breach—i.e. it cannot admit that the idea of an unsurpassable being is, in addition to being an idea, a real experience of God. And this, in fact, seems to have been the case with St. Anselm and Descartes, with this difference, however, that the experience Anselm required came from faith, and Descartes' came from reason alone. But then if the idea of God is the translation of a lived experience, the *argument* no longer has reason for existence; it does not prove the *existence* of God (a fact already given), but at most his *necessary* existence.

2. *The affirmation of being does not immediately imply the notion of divinity*

The ontological argument presumes that one can pass from the idea of God to the affirmation of his existence. Ontologism can thus be described as the attempt to pass immediately from the experience of being to its divine significance. Ontologism places perception of being at the source of knowledge: every judgment on our part presupposes at least a confused intuition that being " exists. " Perceived in this manner, being is necessarily infinite: it could not be defined otherwise, since it is contrasted with existents which are all finite. Thus the affirmation of being gets its meaning only in the idea of a divine being.

The error of this concept is not so much in the fact that it presupposes at the very outset some kind of contact between the mind and absolute being, for " in him we live, and move, and are. " (If " God is within all " [Eph 4,6], he is also and more especially in the mind). Rather it lies in the fact that this supposed contact can give way to an *objective*, *actual* perception and therefore the intellect can immediately understand the *absolute meaning* of Being. This is a gross error about the connatural object of the intellect. What immediate experience teaches us is not that *being is* (or subsists) but that *beings are*. Human reason does not grasp being except by means of created things. Finite being or existence can be conceived by man only from finite essences. Now the meaning or reason of being is not contained in the reason of any finite essence, which only means that the human mind does not have evidence of *esse purum*, God. The fact of God's existence perhaps constitutes some kind of evidence for some infinite intellect, but not for man. Perhaps the mind is in contact with divine being from its birth—let us grant this to the ontologists—still it does not know him, for the meaning of pure being escapes it. In order to know something about pure being, the mind *proceeds by means of* beings; it must see them as the effects of a cause, and this involves a reasoning process and not simply perception from evidence. If human reason would be deprived of an *immediate intuition* of being and would use only an *abstract* knowledge of the nature of things, all intuition of God would be impossible. A reasoning process is needed in order to prove the existence of God: and in the absence of reasoning, the existence of God remains a *problem*. [7]

The same must be said of the act of creation, considered in its cause, and more especially of the act by which God reveals himself. It is too easily thought to be sufficient to say that God makes himself known in the act and fact of revelation. The very act of revelation is not so compelling. Since it is given to us by a *witness*, revelation presupposes a knowledge of a truth-speaking God who cannot deceive or be deceived. But the existence of a truth-speaking God is not evident.

Conclusion

A dialogue is therefore necessary in order to arrive at an authentic knowledge of God, and faith does not free man from his responsibility in this regard. Even faith requires a certain " thought " process. Is such a conclusion disconcerting? Why does the Church distrust ontologism? In order to understand the reason, one must emphasize the dangerous ambiguity of a doctrine which pretends to evidence in our knowledge of God. There is no doubt that ontologism favors religious sentiment because of this bias. Yet it has also often been the case that pious souls have replaced their life of faith by a new approach based on evidence. The consequence of such a tendency is that with the impoverishment of any mystery, distrust of the human condition and the laws of its progress sets in. In knowledge wherein everything is positive, clear, evident, there is no longer any place for the " slow, painful, and patient work of

---

[7] We would still have to investigate the possibility of a subjective experience of God by reflection, which turns the soul in upon its own existence and then upon God, who is more intimate to the soul than the soul is to itself. In this regard, cf. the enlightening chapter by Jacques Maritain, " L'expérience mystique naturelle et le vide, " in *Quatre essais sur l'esprit dans sa condition charnelle* (Desclée de Brouwer, 1939) pp. 131-80. Maritain concludes that such an experience, if it is at all possible, could only be *negative* and therefore incapable of *deducing* God's existence from the soul.

negation. " Religious knowledge hovers above time like the platonic idea; it is no longer associated with the difficult path which the human journey must follow, nor is it affected by the sufferings of this world. Finally it is not confronted with the problematic state of human knowledge since it denies that the existence of God is a problem. It is therefore a knowledge by which man escapes from his very own history . . . .

§ II. The Existence of God Is Demonstrable

I. THE TEACHING OF FAITH

Is it at all possible, without any evidence, to attain to a knowledge of God by a rational process? What does revelation say about this?

1. *Sacred Scripture*

1) *The Old Testament.* In the Old Testament, the most explicit testimony is found in the Book of Wisdom. Writing for men imbued with Greek culture, the author appeals to their intellect in order to deter them from the worship of idols. How can any sensible man be ignorant of the true nature of " him who is " while deifying what is nothing else but a force or element of nature, when nature itself gives evidence of the existence of an infinitely perfect Creator? Actually, it is clear that the Master of the universe surpasses in beauty the things he has created: " Since through the grandeur and beauty of the creatures we may, by analogy, contemplate their Author " (Wis 13,5). The existence of an all-good and all-powerful God is thus accessible to reason, if it begins with visible things; this is what the sacred writer wants to say. He does not care to enter into the details of the demonstration; he leaves this consideration to the philosopher. At most he indicates in a general way that it is possible, by some process of deduction (v. 4) to pass from natural perfections to supreme perfection. There is a certain relationship of proportion between creature and creator, an " analogy " such as we recognize between *more* and *less*. The key word *(analógōs)* evokes the idea of a relationship, of a comparison which is given to us by nature herself; if such are his works, how much far superior must be the Master!

2) *St. Paul* takes up the teaching of the Book of Wisdom but places it in radically new perspective. Natural knowledge of God is treated in relation to salvation by faith. All men need redemption brought by Christ, because all, Jews and pagans, are equally under the domination of sin, though not in the same way. The somber moral degradation into

which the pagans are plunged can be summarized in one word: idolatry. They have adored and served the creature instead of the Creator. Such an error is inexcusable; it is a sin: " for what can be known about God is perfectly plain to them since God himself has made it plain. Ever since God created the world his everlasting power and deity, however invisible, have been there for the mind to see in the things he has made. So they are without excuse: they knew God and yet refused to honor him as God or to thank him " (Rom 1,19-21). This form of reasoning clearly reveals the principle underlying St. Paul's thought: the pagans ignored this knowledge of God and this enveloped them in culpable ignorance instead of opening them, as it should have done, to the revelation of salvation in Christ Jesus.

Notice that the affirmation of a natural knowledge of God comes as proof of an accusation: culpable ignorance which is reproached in the pagans presupposes that a certain knowledge of God is possible if one begins from creatures. In any other case the accusation of idolatry would not be justified. The pagans have acquired this knowledge in a given moment: not only does all of creation constitute objectively a permanent manifestation of divine perfections, but men have known how to decode its message. " They know God, " says Paul quite clearly. Yet the same Apostle holds no less categorically that " they do not know God " (1 Thess 4,5; 2 Thess 1,8; Gal 4,8; 1 Cor 1,21). This contradiction is characteristic of his thought.

What does it mean? It is possible that the Apostle had in mind an historical failure, viz., that wicked men of his century had replaced the truly religious folk of earlier times. But it seems that his thought goes further. He takes for granted in these men a certain kind of " monstrous coexistence, " [8] of the knowledge of God and the error of idolatry. How to explain this phenomenon? These pagans are neither entirely correct nor entirely in error. They do not know God. It makes no difference that these pagans have no *explicit* knowledge of God. A simple reflection upon their behavior reveals that their idolatry necessarily would be shattered even on the basis of an incomplete but true knowledge of God. Truth is not dead, it is only " obscured, " held " captive " by injustice. The injustice of idolatry is the tyrannical domination of ingratitude over truth. This state of affairs constitutes ignorance of God. In our day we would say that the pagans are in " bad faith. " " If then by natural knowledge of God is understood not the religious pagan conscience in its historical form, but the secret knowledge which idolatry itself includes and reflection

---

[8] J. Dupont, *Gnosis* (Louvain-Paris, 1949) p. 30.

uncovers therein, then we must admit that Paul recognized the actual existence of this natural knowledge in the pagans. " [9]

One must not believe, however, that in the thought of St. Paul natural knowledge plays only a negative role, one of accusation. It also plays a positive role. The accusation demands a reversal: the need to " seek God " (Acts 17,27) weighs heavily upon men. In fact, the Apostle waits for the pagans to " turn from these empty idols to the living God who made heaven and earth and the sea and all that these hold " (Acts 14,15; 1 Thess 1,9). Certainly the Apostle had no intention at all of developing a natural theology. When he declares to the Athenians, " The God whom I proclaim is in fact the one whom you already worship without knowing it " (Acts 17,23), he does not seek to re-establish any kind of natural religion. Yet it would be wrong to believe that revelation censures all natural knowledge of God as vain. It is still necessary even in the Christian era. Without it man could not be conscious of the sin of idolatry, nor could he repent (Acts 17,30); without it he could no longer trust in a true and truth-speaking God, nor consequently could he believe in him of whom God " has given assurance to all men by raising him from the dead " (Acts 17,31). It is through a true knowledge of God that man is open to revelation.

2. *The teaching of the Fathers*

The Fathers refer to these classical passages of Scripture in an invariable manner, whether they seek to redress the pagan errors as do, e.g., the Apologists, [10] Tertullian, [11] St. Athanasius, [12] or whether they propose on the contrary to beat down the excesses of the gnostics (as e.g. St. Irenaeus [13]) or the claims of Eunomius by use of immediate evidence (as e.g. the Cappadocian Fathers [14]). Basically, the doctrine remains the same: by means of a reasoning process that begins with creatures, one can affirm the existence of God. The point of departure may vary, and

[9] H. Bouillard, *Karl Barth* III, p. 122.

[10] Athenagoras, *Leg. pro Chr.*, 4, *PG* 6, 897. — Minucius Felix, *Octavius*, c. 17, *PL* 3, 286; c. 32, *PL* 3, 341. — St. Theophilus, *Ad Autolycum*, I, 5, *PG* 6, 1031.

[11] Tertullian, *Apol.* 17, *PL* 1, 375.

[12] Athanasius, *Or. Contra Gentes*, 27, 30, 34, 43, *PG* 25, 54, 59, 68, 86.

[13] St. Irenaeus, *Adv. Haer.*, 2, 6, 1; 2, 9, 1; 4, 6, 6; *PG* 7, 124, 734, 989.

[14] St. Basil, *Adv. Eunomium*, I, 14, *PG* 29, 544; *Epist.* 235, *PG* 32, 872. — Gregory of Nazianzen, *Orationes*, 28, 6, *PG* 36, 32. — Gregory of Nyssa, *Contra Eunomium*, 12, *PG* 45, 985. Cf. also St. John Chrysostom, *De incomprehensibili*, 5, 5, *PG* 48, 743.

appeal can be made to the physical universe, or the human soul which is created in the image of God, or to the moral conscience. Each one of these ways leads in sure fashion to knowledge of some perfection of God. The only ones who go astray are those who lack the required moral disposition, as St. Paul has shown.

3. *The doctrine of the Church*

The Church has solemnly defined its faith at the First Vatican Council. It had to take a position against a twofold heresy: *agnosticism*, which denied reason the possibility of proving God's existence; and *fideism*, which demanded divine revelation as necessary in order to prove God's existence. According to the definitions of the Council, it is heretical to say that " the one and true God, our creator and lord, cannot be known with certainty with the natural light of human reason by means of the things that have been made "(Sess. III, Cap. 2, Can. 1, Denz 1806). The chapter preceding this canon furnishes more details on its true meaning. The natural knowledge which is mentioned bears upon the existence of God; this is the defined truth. But it is not defined that creation, which evokes the title " creator, " is demonstrable. As to the *quality* of this knowledge, it is " certain. " The Fathers have no doubt deliberately avoided the words " *demonstrare*, " " *probare*, " but they have maintained the word " *certo*. " Thus there is no question here of a mere probability or probable opinion.

The Council however affirms the *possibility* of this knowledge and not the fact of its existence; the statement therefore makes no allusion to any specifics. As to the *means* to be used, from the *subjective* point of view this would be the light of reason: i.e. a *personal* power, which would not exclude the necessity of education, and a *natural* power, capable of being exercised independently of any supernatural help, without for all that denying the possibility of a revelation. It is known moreover that the Council expounded the moral necessity of divine revelation for the majority of men. This divine revelation of the existence of God is justified only because of the plan of God to call all men to a supernatural destiny. [15]

[15] The First Vatican Council adopted the views of St. Thomas: " Even as regards those truths about God which human reason could have discovered, it was necessary that man should be taught by a divine revelation; because the truth about God such as reason could discover would only be known by a few, and that after a long time, and with the admixture of many errors. Whereas man's whole salvation, which is in God, depends upon the knowledge of this truth. Therefore, in order that the salvation of men might be brought about more fitly and more surely, it was necessary that they should be taught divine truth by divine revelation. " *Summa Theologica* I, 1, 1.

Finally, the Council specifies the *objective* means that lead to certain knowledge of God: these are all creatures, visible or invisible. Augustinian or Cartesian-type proofs are not at all rejected by this position. [16] Innatism is not even considered, since it admits that contact with creatures is necessary for awakening in us the idea of God. The sum total of doctrine thus defined amounts to a simple explanation of the verses of the Epistle to the Romans (1,18-20), which might be consulted to good advantage; but the Council never intended to define the fuller sense of this text.

The teaching of the Council will be taken up again and confirmed by the encyclicals *Aeterni Patris* and *Pascendi*, then made explicit in the *Oath Against Modernism*. This latter not only states that God can be known with certitude, but that his existence can be demonstrated with the aid of visible things, " as a cause from its effect " (Denz 2145). It should be understood, however, that there is no endorsement of any particular metaphysics by the use of the words " demonstration, " " cause, " " effect. " Furthermore, there is no question here of a *de fide* definition, but rather as Pius XI called it in his encyclical *Studiorum ducem*, this is an " interpretation " of the First Vatican Council. The Oath formulates a profession of faith, yet only a temporary one, and it has not been imposed on the universal Church. In our own days, Pope Pius XII has maintained, against some tendencies of contemporary theology, that no one should doubt that " the human reason, unaided by God's revelation and by his grace, can really prove the existence of a personal God by inference from the facts of creation. "

Thesis II. *Deus unus et verus, creator et Dominus noster, per ea quæ facta sunt, naturali lumine, certo cognosci potest* (de fide definita); *adeoque tamquam causam per effectus demonstrari potest* (doctrina communis).

The one and true God, our creator and lord, can be known with certainty with the natural light of human reason by means of things that have been made *(defined of faith);* his existence can also be demonstrated as a cause from its effect *(common doctrine).*

---

[16] J. Maritain, *Distinguish to Unite or the Degrees of Knowledge*, tr. by Gerald B. Phelan (New York: Scribner's Sons, 1959) pp. 222-26. Cf. also J. Maritain, *Approches de Dieu* (Paris: Aubier, 1960) pp. 81-93; and E. Gilson, " L'avenir de la métaphysique augustinienne, " *Rev. de Phil.* (1931) pp. 367-68; 373-77; 381-84.

II. THE UNDERSTANDING OF FAITH

1. *The nature of demonstration*

Let us begin with the most explicitly defined point in the teaching of the Church. How can the proposition: " God's existence is demonstrable " be explained theologically? In order to dispose of the most serious objections, the unique character of the demonstration of God's existence must be pointed out. The Church herself prepares us for this by determining the nature of this reasoning: a demonstration of a cause from its effects. In this way every form of reasoning based on the understanding of " why " is eliminated: e.g. Peter speaks, because he is a man. In such reasoning, the middle term, *man*, represents both the logical and ontological cause of the final conclusion: it permits one to conclude not only *that* Peter can speak, but it tells *why:* because he is a man. It is evident that the conclusion that God exists could never be achieved with this type of an argument, for God has no cause. God does not exist *because* he creates the world, nor even in order to create the world. The question: Why does God exist, makes no sense.

Yet it is possible to conceive a form of reasoning that is less pretentious, leading from the observation of a fact to the affirmation of " its reason, " yet without entering into the understanding of this " reason "—e.g. " Peter, *by the fact* that he speaks, is a man. " The conclusion would appear to be a necessary and immediate result of the premises (every being that speaks and converses is a man) and yet the means used, the word, represents in the ontological order not a cause but an effect: word is a property of human nature. Such reasoning gives certitude, but it does not tell " why " man is essentially what he is. We thus have the elements with which to explain, at least remotely, the reasoning that affirms that God exists. If it is possible to conceive of the world as an effect, we could say *by analogy* that God who produced the world also exists, just as anyone who speaks a word is a man. The means of the demonstration (the universe) is posited as an effect of this cause which is God. The world *exists* because God *exists* as the cause of the world—even though we do not know what God is.

2. *The point of departure for the demonstration*

It suffices to follow the course of such reasoning to see that the world is an effect. This seems difficult to very keen minds, but everyone is aware of Kant's famous statement: it does not follow from all the causality that we see *in* the world, that there is a causality *of* the world. The objection has the merit of emphasizing the fact that the words *effect* and *cause* can express different levels of reality. In order to remove all ambiguity, it is important to reflect closely upon the meaning of these terms; the proof for the existence of God will then appear in all its originality.

Etymologically, the word " effect " comes from " *facio* "—to make or to do; it signifies that which is the final result of a cause and independent of it, the product of a certain activity. Yet diverse effects lead to diverse ways of understanding the nature of a cause.

The effect can first of all be the result of a very human *praxis*. A watch is produced by a watchmaker. The watch can be termed an " effect " when it is observed that the materials used (brass, steel, rubies, etc.) are something entirely different from the final product; their assemblage is the effect of a cause. But can we conclude from the fact that the world, considered in its totality, is *an effect*, and say that just as it requires a watchmaker to make a watch, *so too* it was necessary that God make the universe? Obviously not, if " so too " is understood in a univocal sense; for the existence of products of work in the world does not necessarily imply that the world itself is a product of work performed by a transcendent cause. A closer investigation can show quite clearly that human *praxis*, from beginning to end, *presupposes* the existence of the world and operates in these conditions which cannot be duplicated for the world itself, nor for the cause of this world, if one does exist.

Equally deceptive conclusions would be reached by considering solely the level of *nature*. Nature could be considered from one point of view as effect: that which is born, that which appears at the end of an evolution as the effect of a much more mysterious work than simple human labor. Still the question raised by this evolution does not force us to go beyond this world, if it is only a question of very accurately explaining the " becoming " of things that exist in the world. *What is it* that " becomes " or " progresses " if not the world, considered as a subject of development or becoming? *What* does it " become " or " develop into " if not a certain form or complexus which in other words is the world considered in its form or structure? And *whence* does it come if not from the ensemble of anterior causes which have cooperated in its formation? In brief, any questions that might be raised by a scholar regarding the evolution of the world can be reduced to principles or explanations or causes immanent in the universe. Whence comes man? From his father, answers Marx; and he is correct if nothing else is considered except the *development* of generations. From all development in the world, it still does not follow that the world must be in its totality the term of a development whose initial principle would be God.

If then the evolution of the world does not oblige the savant to recur immediately to a transcendent cause, what can be said of the very *existence* of a world in evolution? Why is there a world in evolution at all? While we investigate that which is presupposed in every activity and movement of things, namely the simple fact of existence, are we finally going to perceive the world as effect? We must proceed here with prudence. To perceive a thing as effect presupposes that one is astonished by it: the mind is stunned by what it sees, as if it faced an unusual or abnormal situation. It is important to grasp the reason for this astonishment which forces a person to regard the world as an effect. *A priori*, the fact that a thing *might exist*, in no way at all forces one to consider it automatically as an effect or cause. Recall in this regard the embarrassing question of Bergson: why be astonished that the world might exist, rather than that it might not exist? Is it not more natural and less astonishing that the world might exist rather than not? Heidegger makes this pertinent observation: " After two-and-a-half thousand years it would seem to be about time to consider what the Being of being has to do with such things as principles and causes. " [17]

Is it necessary to develop the question of the existence of existents in relation to questions on the causality of the world? There are two ways of resolving the problem of causality once and for all. If one is satisfied simply to view the phenomena which manifest the essence or structure of the world without going so far as to investigate the very fact of its existence, it is useless to raise the problem of its absolute origin. As Aristotle already noted, to ask why a man is a man (or why the world is such as it is) is a superfluous question. Yet in order to keep a clear conscience, we must put aside the very existence of the world for awhile.

If, however, one is satisfied with viewing only the pure fact of existence, without considering the existents which manifest it (if that were possible) recourse to causality would once again be senseless: for the question of being obviously touches upon the problem of causality. The world could not appear as effect unless it were understood as an " existent-world " in the unity of its essence and existence. Valéry writes that the astonishing fact is not that things exist or do not exist, but that they are such and not other. Pure being, or nothing, causes no problem; in fact, it leaves us quite unmoved. But the fact that being only appears to human eyes in a modified, diversified, and arbitrary form in the existents of this world—this is the core of the problem. The mind would like to see being

[17] M. Heidegger, *What is Philosophy?*, tr. with an introd. by William Kluback and Jean T. Wilde (Twayne Publishers, Inc., 1948) p. 57.

itself, but what it actually does see is a diversity of existents. Specifically, what really raises this problem of causality—as will be shown later on—is the tension between existence and existents. The intellect perceives in a confused manner that the meaning of existence is one of relationship to existents. The absence of identity between existents and existence is precisely the element that allows us to view the world as an effect. Still we must resolutely take a metaphysical point of view.

§ III.   The Affirmation of God's Existence Is True

Although the existence of God is not evident, it is demonstrable by human reason. This, at least, is what we believe on faith. Nevertheless, even though the Church grants to human reason the possibility of attaining some kind of knowledge of God, it teaches nothing about human reason *actually* having constructed some rigorously certain demonstrations. And this is why it is necessary, from a theologian's point of view, to show the fittingness of this aptitude, even if it has not yet been verified in reality. In undertaking such verification, we proceed from the possibility to the fact—a method which would indeed be questioned in philosophy, but which has value in theology.

The statements that God's existence is demonstrable and that God's existence can be demonstrated by this or that specific method are for the theologian two distinct truths which do not have the same importance when considered from the point of view of certitude of faith. The theologian undertakes a demonstration at his own risk. He expects to be questioned both by philosophers and theologians, but his project is undebatable, for what he does, he does out of obedience to the faith in trying to elaborate and develop the possibilities suggested by this same faith. On the other hand he acts with the intention of acquiring an understanding of the faith which has set him this goal. Actually, faith leaves no doubt concerning the orientation that demonstration should take, or about the possibility of proceeding towards God without leaving the realm of existence, or finally, the kind of demonstration that can ultimately affirm the *existence* of God.

I.   THE TEACHING OF FAITH

The revealed word serves as a guide for the theologian. " God is " is true because this affirmation echoes the statement of him who one day told Moses: " I am who I am... this is my name forever, and thus am I to be remembered throughout all generations " (Ex 3,14-15).

1. *The name of Yahweh*

The interpretation of the name of Yahweh has long been debated. It is generally agreed that this word is a form of the verb *hawah*, which means " to be, " in the simplest sense of the word: " And God said, ' let there be light '; and there was light " (Gen 1,3). But exegetes are divided on the meaning to be given to this name of Yahweh. Two quite complementary interpretations seem to stand out. [18]

1) According to the first interpretation, the name of Yahweh expresses the behavior or conduct of God toward his people. Actually, God revealed his name and the role he willed to play for his people in a specific historical situation. He also revealed his name for the purpose of establishing a relationship with his chosen people. He revealed his name, so that he might be invoked and put at the disposal of his people all his power and mercy, and thereby render himself close to them. In brief, he wanted to establish an everlasting covenant with them. The name ought to be invoked, therefore, because it expresses this relationship, this promise: " You will be my people, and I, I am, i.e. I am for you, and with you. " We have a proof of this interpretation *a contrario:* when the people turned away from God, the covenant was temporarily announced in the following manner: " Call his name ' Not my people, ' for you are not my people and I am not your God " (Hos 1,9). In this context, the name of God appears at the basis of the covenant, it gives expression to it: God is present here as the Master of life and death, the Master of human destiny and the Saviour: " See now that I, I am he, and there is no god beside me; I kill and I make alive... " (Deut 32,39).

2) But this first meaning presupposes another, more fundamental one. It is not only in the Bible that God is the Master of life and death, the Lord of history; he truly is the living and eternal God. He is not limited simply to sustaining things in existence. True, he doesn't need creatures in order to exist: he is. His life is internal to himself. That is why other exegetes think with good reason that they recognize in the text from Exodus a revelation from God about himself, absolutely speaking, and not only about God in his historical activity. In regard to his people, God could exist, or not exist, but in himself he does exist

---

[18] In addition let us also mention the thesis held by W. F. Albright, *From Stone Age to Christianity,* according to whom one would have to see the causative form (hiphil) in the name YHWH and render it " He causes to be or exist. " Some objections, however, could be raised: 1) linguistic arguments are not decisive; 2) the Hebrew vocabulary contained other more precise words to express creative action. This is the opinion of E. Dhorme who, having held this belief for a while, finally rejected it. Cf. " Le Nom du Dieu d'Israël, " *RHR* 91 (1952) 17.

eternally. Yahweh thus means above all that God exists; " he is " in
the strongest sense of the word. Other gods do not exist and no creature
is like him. He is the One-who-is, this is his proper character, and
consequently, this is his name.

No particular metaphysics is directly endorsed by this revelation,
and the name is not an abstract definition, it is very clear. The verbal
structure of the name indicates that it is not a *defined representation*, but
an *affirmation* of the indefinable; he is. Any representation of what he
is can only be misleading. In order to know God truly, one must cast
from one's mind every image, every idol *(eidōlon)*, every wooden or stone
or imaginary representation, carved according to human dimensions. In
this regard the very exacting prescriptions of the covenant are a logical
consequence to the revelation made at Horeb, where " Yahweh spoke to
you from the midst of the fire; you heard the sound of words, but saw
no shape; there was only a voice " (Deut 4,12). The voice said: I am,
and the faithful understood: he is, without beginning or end, equal to
the burning inextinguishable flame which kindled the bush on the desert
sands.

2. *Hebrew thought*

The evolution of Hebrew thought from Moses to St. John confirms this
twofold interpretation.

During the Babylonian Captivity, the author of the *Book of
Consolation* saw no better reason for hope than the very name of God:
he is. Hope legitimately remains because God is called Yahweh; this
is the author's basic argument. *Because* God is called Yahweh, he exists,
without beginning or end, the first and last (41,4; 44,6; 48,12). Because
such is his name, it is he who has created everything, he is the absolute
Master of things and beings, the Lord of the Universe; except for him,
nothing exists, everything else is naught (45,14-21; 46,9). It is thus
evident that the name of Yahweh involves what already might be called
a theology; for to this basic revelation the author adds the affirmation
of God's eternity, unity, omnipotence, and fidelity. Far from restricting
the meaning of the name to the act of creation, he contrasts it, so to speak,
with the result of creation: God exists, the creature does not .... [19]

The author of the *Book of Wisdom* does not hesitate to designate
God as He-who-is *(ton ónta)*, with this specification, that one can attain
knowledge of him who is by means of a rational process, independently
of revelation which is the basis of the covenant (Wis 13,1ff).

[19] E. Boismard, " Le Dieu des Exodes, " *Lumière et Vie* 3 (1952) 115.

3. *The Gospel of John*

St. John's gospel mentions the name of God many times but with a new intention. There no longer is any question of knowing who God is; that doctrine is already established. The question now is, who is Jesus Christ? Christ takes upon himself the name of God: I am. In addition, just as in the previous revelations, the expression *Ego eimi* states at one and the same time what Christ is in himself and what he is for all men. When the phrase precedes the announcement of a title, it indicates the nature of the mission that Christ came to fulfill among men (I am the Bread, the Light, the Gate, the Good Shepherd, the Resurrection, the Way, the Truth and the Life, the Vine). When the phrase appears alone it affirms his divinity as, e.g. in the celebrated reply to his detractors: "I tell you most solemnly, before Abraham ever was, I am" (Jn 8,58). Note in this passage that the expression *Ego eimi* implies not only a temporal pre-existence: Christ does not say: I was before Abraham, but I am before Abraham. The nonsequence of tenses indicates that here it is a question of a nontemporal pre-existence. The being of Christ is situated in an absolute sphere which transcends time. We must even go further: the transcendence of Christ over history is declared as an ontological transcendence. The difference between eternity in which Christ exists and time in which Abraham's life unfolded is an ontological difference, the same which distinguishes *genestai* from *einai*. Such is the view (it could be called metaphysical) that John's concept of the divinity of Christ demands. Already in his prologue where a similar contrast is seen, *einai* was carefully reserved for the Word, and *genestai*, for creatures. Chapter VIII gives us the reason for this: the affirmation of absolute existence applies only to God. [20]

4. *The teaching of the Fathers*

The teaching of the Fathers on the interpretation of the name of Yahweh remained unchanged. Whatever their doctrinal differences might have been, they agreed on the principles. To the question, "Who is God?" they have but one answer: God is He who is. From St. Irenaeus to St. John of Damascus the phrase is repeated indefinitely. [21] The meaning

---

[20] Cf. E. Schweitzer, *Ego eimi* (Göttingen, 1939) and Kunsin, *Charakter und Ursprung der johannischen Reden* (Riga, 1939).

[21] In regard to the Greek and Oriental Fathers, cf.: Irenaeus, *Adv. Haer.*, 3, 6, 2, *PG* 7, 861. — Clement of Alexandria, *Paedagogus*, *PG* 8, 336; *Stromata*, 6, 16, *PG* 9, 364. — Origen, *Com. in Jn.*, *PG* 14, 136. — Eusebius, *Praeparatio evangelica*, 9-10, *PG* 21, 868-73. — Ephrem, *Adv. Haereses*, *AS* 2, 555. — Athanasius, *De decretis*, *PG* 25, 456. — Gregory of Nazianzen, *Oratio* 30, *PG* 36, 125-28. — Gregory

of this phrase is not at all doubted; the Fathers are unaware of the evasive sense proposed by some modern exegetes; nor do they recognize the causative.   With the exception of Denis, whose negative theology is sense inspired by the philosophy of Plato's *Parmenides*, the name revealed to Moses has an absolute and positive meaning for them.   More precisely, it constitutes the proper name of God.   In this specific regard the Fathers surpass everything that the Greek philosophers had been able to teach about God.   One cannot find in Plato or in Aristotle the teaching that anything characteristic of God should be considered in terms of absolute being.   For the Fathers, on the other hand, who believe in one God and to whom the Bible revealed his name, only he is called *God* who had said to Moses, " I am who I am "—and conversely when God is named, only he is called God who *truly is* God. [22]

God alone exists; that is his proper name, and he shares it with no one else.   Creatures represent " that which does not exist, " even though the Creator has put them into existence.   In order to note the difference that separates creatures from the creator, an important distinction— following the lead of Origen—is proposed: creatures are not being, they only receive being; they do not exist by nature, they exist by the will of God who sustains them in their existence.

God, however, exists by nature, [23] and that is why he to the exclusion of every other existent deserves to be called he who is.   The Fathers conclude from this that the name means more than just a quality proper to God: some will go so far as to say that this name signifies his substance, or nature. [24]   The essence of God obviously remains incomprehensible, but it is enunciated by this name as a property of the word itself.

---

of Nyssa, *Contra Eunomium*, *PG* 45, 768-69. — Theodore of Mopsuestia, *Hom. Cat.* 2, 9 (éd. R. M. Tonneau, p. 41). — Cyril of Alexandria, *In Is. comm.*, 4, 2, *PG* 70, 924. — John of Damascus, *De fide orthodoxa* I, 9, *PG* 94, 836. — Among the Latin Fathers consult: Tertullian, *Adv. Praxean*, 17, *PL* 2, 176. — Hilary, *De Trinitate*, I, 5, *PL* 10, 28. — Ambrose, *In Ps.* 43 *ennar.*, *PL* 14, 1100, *Epistola* 8, *PL* 16, 914. — Jerome, *In Ep. ad Eph.*, 2, 3, *PL* 26, 488. — Augustine, *In Jn. ev. tr.* 28, 8, 8-10, *PL* 35, 1678-79, *Ennar. in Ps.* 121, 5, *PL* 37, 1621, *Ennar. in Ps.* 134, *PL* 37, 1741. (Cf. also E. Gilson, *Philosophie et incarnation selon saint Augustin* (Montreal, 1947) p. 26, n. 1) — Bernard, *De consideratione*, 5, 6, *PL* 182, 795-96.

[22] E. Gilson, *The Spirit of Mediaeval Philosophy*, tr. by A. A. C. Downes (New York: C. Scribner's Sons, 1936) pp. 42-63.

[23] Origen, *In Libr. I Reg. Hom I, ii*, *PG* 12, 1008-09. Gregory of Nyssa, *De vita Moyse*, I, *PG* 44, 333 A.

[24] Ephrem, Gregory of Nazianzen, Gregory of Nyssa, John of Damascus Hilary, cf. note 21 above.

Important in itself, the knowledge of God is even more important for the developments to which it gives rise. The Fathers (especially the Latin Fathers) deduce his eternity from the revelation made to Moses, and in this way they remain faithful to the inspiration of the author of the *Book of Consolation.*

Another remarkable consequence deals with the divinity of Christ. The declaration made by Jesus in St. John's gospel, "Before Abraham was, I am," has been steadily interpreted as testimony to the pre-existence of Christ and thus has been related to his divinity, since eternal existence belongs only to God. Equally evident has been the interest stirred by the theology of the divine name as a basis for the doctrine of creation. Since God alone possesses existence by nature, creatures can only gain it by participation. In regard to evil, when it is reduced to non-being, it is actually no work of God. Only participated being has its cause in God, the supreme Good: that is the line followed by Origen, [25] and this doctrine is also based on the revelation of Exodus.

5. *First Vatican Council*

This is the God whom the First Vatican Council had in mind, the God revealed to the prophets in Jesus Christ, when it condemned those who denied the existence of the true God. One must be careful not to diminish the bearing and importance of the anathema: it includes only those who dare to deny the existence of all divinity but also those who obstinately refuse to see a true God in the God of Christianity, even though like the deists they recognize some supreme divinity. Such a rationalism must be condemned in the same breath with atheism in the strict sense of the word.

Thesis III. *Dicit Dominus: Ego* The Lord said: I am who I am.
sum qui sum.

II. THE UNDERSTANDING OF FAITH

The believer holds the existence of God as true because of his act of faith in the word of God. For the theologian who seeks to understand this word, the question comes down to this: can the fact of " *being*" assume

[25] Origen, *Com. in Jn. II,* 7, *PG* 14, 136.

an *absolute* or divine meaning?   So long as the very *meaning* of being is not discovered, we cannot judge how God might be conceived in the language of being.

The question also cannot be resolved by an appeal to evidence.   We do not see being itself; we see only that this thing exists, that everything exists.   This indicates that the meaning of being will be uncovered only by reflecting upon the things at our disposal.   Reason will therefore proceed in the following manner: (1) the totality of things which constitute our universe exist, or rather they exercise the *act of existence (esse)*; (2) now in point of fact, analysis proves that from the metaphysical point of view, these things represent a deficiency in being (as well as in intelligibility).   They do not exist of themselves, but rather by participation, since no one of them is identical with its act of existence or being.   Therefore they exist by an Other and this Other, in order to be their *Cause*, must exist by himself or by essence; (3) whence it can be concluded that this Cause exists.   The existence of God will thus have been manifest, not in itself, but in a very simple way, from the viewpoint of a causality acting upon the world.   Let us take up each detail of the steps of this argument.

I.   THE WORLD AS EXISTING

The demonstration of the existence of God can be put in a nutshell in the affirmation that this world exists.   One question alone suffices to develop this statement: what is the meaning of the fact of being an existent, or simply of existing? [26]

1.   *Transcendence of esse*

As a matter of fact, the starting point for reflection in the unveiling of being remains narrowly limited: it can manifest being only by investigating being in relation to particular existents—by asking, e.g. " what meaning does the word being have for a fire, a child, a home, and in a general way, for all things that *exist?* "   The baffling element in such a question is that

[26] The term " being " can often be ambiguous in translation since it can signify a noun (*ens* - a being) or a verb (*esse* - the act of existence). To avoid misunderstanding, *ens* will be translated " existent, " and *esse* will be translated " existence. " The word " being " will be used in all other cases where the context renders its meaning quite clear and unmistakable. Strictly speaking, *existere* means *ex-alio-sistere* (to exist by participation in another being) and connotes the idea of a beginning. In this sense, God does not exist, he is. Practically speaking, this distinction is entirely overlooked in this treatise. It is not of momentous import to the subject.

it seeks no particular answer. We ask that question about everything: what *is* this? Being is the basis of every question.

Specifically, in allowing the possibility of investigating everything, the question of being expresses the desire for a knowledge, the possession of which will furnish the total explanation for everything that exists. But the knowledge considered by this basic question is both prefigured and hidden by particular questions which are related, e.g. to the doctor, the psychologist, the sociologist, etc. Each of the explanations provided by these respective sciences aims, in its own right, at presenting fire, the child, the home, *such as* they are, and together they help us understand *what* they are. But it must be noted that scientific knowledge, just like the technical knowledge which derives from it, always implicitly *presupposes* the very presence of these things; the mind's attention is not yet drawn by the pure fact that they *exist or are.*

2. *The universality of esse or the act of existing*

To feel the attraction of being no longer means to think only of *what* things are, or what can be *done* with them, but to take into account that by which they are *actually present.* By allowing ourselves to be drawn by the revelation of being in existents, we become involved in a domain which surpasses by far this or that particular existent. The knowledge gained from this manifestation of being is a knowledge which corresponds to the intelligibility of everything that exists, for *everything* does exist, everything is actually present. Being is that by which things are present to me with a total presence, this means that in all things being can be placed at the end of an act of knowledge, for its *logos (reason)* is such that it assures the assembly and the coherence of everything into *one* world.

3. *The actuality of esse or the act of existing*

But there is a question here of a very special kind of knowledge. It is clear that the intelligibility of being presently under consideration could not be reduced to the idea of a genus, whose comprehension would be as small as its extension would be great. In removing, by abstraction, that which makes a child, a child, fire, fire, a home, a home, one ultimately arrives at the idea of an existent, common to every existent *(ens commune).* Yet as a matter of fact, the idea of an existent which we develop in conceiving these above items is never the equivalent of the existence which they have in themselves. There is an unbridgeable *gap* between " that which exists" and human reason's " knowledge of that which exists. " We are aware of this gap, and the object that remains on the other side is not really unknown, because we speak of it; but we no longer have an abstract knowledge of the individual as it exists outside the mind.   Existence simply cannot be abstracted from that which exists.   That which human reason does abstract from existents is the concept that it forms of their *nature*.   Existence itself cannot be conceptualized. [27]   There is no possible concept of the *act* of existence; this can be signified only by an act of judgment.   Unlike a concept which represents a thing internal to the mind, " judgment is an act which affirms an act: an act of thought which affirms an act of existence. " [28]   Thus the intellect knows existence not in an idea which it would retain, but rather in a *tendency (tension)* toward existence itself, in an *intentio* which is not a representation but an affirmation.   This affirmation is the act by which the intellect both *participates in and becomes aware* of its relation to being, as the act of every act and perfection of every perfection. [29]   The " reason " of being therefore is not this idea with universal extension in which everything would in the long run be reduced to the state of nothingness.   It is rather a fullness, an act which reduces everything, which leads everything back to itself, including thought, by reason of its universal richness.   Everything is in act; everything begins to exist in a manner similar to an orator carried away by his speech, or a lover snatched up in the passion of his love.   All things exist, this is the statement which in its fullness contains all others.

2.   THE WORLD AS EFFECT

I.   *Being, the foundation of all intelligibility*

This affirmation, however, does not suffice to reveal everything else to us. Since being keeps its distance and evades us, its *meaning* also escapes us. We can describe it only by reference to particular existents.   This is what arouses that strange experience which spurs the intellect to seek a cause. On the one hand we see that the existents whose inner meaning we grasp have no meaning outside of their relationship with being; an individual

[27] By the term " concept " I understand the result of the operation by which reason apprehends the nature of a thing, assimilates it by abstraction, and defines it by representing the thing to itself at the end of its act of intellection.   Cf. St. Thomas, *De Potentia*, 8, 1; 9, 5.

[28] E. Gilson, *L'être et l'essence* (Paris, 1948) p. 285. By *affirmation* I understand the operation by which the mind apprehends existence while reflecting upon its act of knowledge and its origin, and expresses this in the verb " *to be.* "   Concerning the difference between the first operation and the judgment of existence, cf. St. Thomas, *De Veritate*, 1, 3.

[29] St. Thomas, *De Potentia*, 7, 2, ad 9.

exists by everything that it is. Without this relationship to being, it would be *nothing* and would therefore have no meaning for human reason. Thus by the very fact that they exist, the realities of this world have a reason for existing and necessarily so, for an existent which would not exist is inconceivable. As Aristotle said: it is one and the same to be a man and to be an existent: he could be nothing else but an existent, nothing else but what he is, for nothing exists on the edge of existence. Consequently whatever exists necessarily has a reason for existence. *" The name of being is taken from the act of existence. "* [30]

2. *The lack of being implied in the ontological distinction*

On the other hand, the greater the distinction between existence and the existent, the less absolute reason for existence does an existent have. It is a fact that being is not identical with a child, a home, or the world in general. No single thing can appropriate existence to itself in such a degree as to become identical with it. But then there follows this immediate consequence: if existence is not identical with *what* things are (essence), its intelligibility is no longer identical with the intelligibility of things. The " reason " or *logos* of existence therefore is not included in the reason of anything of this world. [31] Things strive after the act of existence, as an orator strives to enter entirely into his speech, or as the thinker strives to concentrate on his act of thinking—all in vain! Things will never be identical with the acts of existence; consequently the realities that we see necessarily have a reason for existence (otherwise they could not exist), but they are not identical with their reason for existence (otherwise they would be existence itself). [32]

3. *The necessity of a cause as a requisite for intelligibility*

It is clear that things do not derive from themselves nor from their essence their own reason for existence. This is the result of the distinction between the existent and existence. In reality, this distinction means that there is in each existent nothing else but something a little *less* than the simple act of existence, i.e. deficiency and potency. Each existent by the

---

[30] *Id., De Veritate*, I, I and I, I, ad 3 (replies to the second series of objections).

[31] *Id., De Veritate*, 10, 12.

[32] Even admitting with van Steenberghen (*Dieu caché*, Louvain, 1961, pp. 78-79) that existence and essence are essentially correlative, this does not mean that we are dealing with relative items that are such by essence. Thus the distinction essence-existence (provided that we do not conceive *esse* as an accident!) quite evidently indicates the contingency of the existent which is characterized by this distinction.

finiteness of its essence presents an insufficient reason for existence (*ratio essendi*), and therefore it is imperfect in relationship to some ideal perfection. Furthermore the lack of existence noticed in each existent corresponds to an equal lack of intelligibility, by the fact that its essence cannot manifest the entire *logos* of existence. We are therefore led to this principle: every existent whose essence is distinct from existence (*esse*) no longer exists by essence. And if it no longer exists by essence, it exists because of some one Other than self. Any other explanation would lead to the absurd. But to admit that the existence of the world has no reason would be to admit that it is totally unintelligible, since it would be entirely independent of being. This is contrary to evidence; the world in its essential structure is intelligible; its existence is the light in which we see what it is. If therefore it is unintelligible in itself, it must be intelligible by some Other than self which is its cause. Let us specify that in order to be perfect this cause must exist of itself, i.e. its essence should include the very meaning of existence. It would thus seem than an imperfect existent, a " being with nothing " can only be understood in relationship to a pure, perfect Being, with no admixture of " nothingness, " or any other imperfection. This is the way human reason advances toward this second affirmation: what does not exist of itself, like these existents which we have experienced, is intelligible only in relationship to an Other existing of himself who is their Reason for existence, or Cause.

3. THE AFFIRMATION OF GOD'S EXISTENCE

All that remains to be done now is to draw the conclusion: this cause *exists*. Not only does it exist in my mind, but it exists by itself. Yet we must not lose sight of our starting point: the affirmation of the existence of a world independently of human reason. Now since it is precisely from the point of view of its existence that the world cries out for a cause, this cause must necessarily exist by itself. Certainly every cause does not necessarily have to exist by itself. Consider, for example, a speech prepared in advance by an orator: the ideas which he foresees he will develop are truly the cause of the discourse. They do not however exist in themselves or by themselves. The cause of that which exists insofar as it does exist must necessarily exist by itself. Begun with an existential statement, the demonstration cannot but conclude with an existential statement; everything that exists and does not exist by itself has as its cause him who exists by himself, the pure act of existence, God. The demonstration dovetails on this point with biblical revelation: God is

" He who is. " It dovetails but does not overlap. Human reason left to itself is actually unaware of all the riches contained in this Name, the depths of divinity to be found therein, the plan of salvation which is prepared therein. The discovery, however, by the mind of that which the eye has never seen nor the ear ever heard does not leave reason disconcerted or crushed under the weight of these new revelations. Actually, revelation finds human reason tending in its direction by this statement which really constitutes the grandeur of man: He is.

4. THE DIFFERENT METHODS OF DEMONSTRATION

The demonstration which has just been explained takes on the pattern of a proof given by St. Thomas in his work *On Being and Essence.* [33] To quote Gilson, it represents a sort of " ultimate metaphysical implication " of the other proofs in that it has recourse to the notions of cause and effect in general. [34] But this implication assumes many forms because causality can take on many different aspects.

It suffices to return to the initial affirmation which began the reflection, " This world is an existent, " in order to see these various aspects.

This mysterious term, " existent, " is the *object* which has suddenly caught the mind's attention. Metaphysics teaches that we can give many names to the reality signified by this term, names which would express all its richness. Insofar as a subject exists, it is capable of terminating or perfecting an act of knowledge, love or admiration, or of becoming one with it. To be true, good, beautiful, to possess self-identity constitutes so many general modes of existence. The consequences of such a line of thought for the demonstration of God's existence should be immediately obvious: if in the major of the syllogism the term " existent " can be replaced by others which are convertible with it and thus cause the different modes of existence to vary before the mind's eye, there will be as many proofs as there are general modes of existence, or rather, these proofs will be as so many variations on one musical theme. It is easy to foresee that in the ways thus opened there will be involved proofs raised by the use of eternal truths, the moral need of an absolute Good,

[33] St. Thomas takes this up as his " third way " in his commentary on the gospel of St. John, Prologue, ed. Marietti, n. 5.

[34] E. Gilson, *The Christian Philosophy of St. Thomas Aquinas,* tr. by L. K. Shook (London: Victor Gollancz, Ltd., 1957) pp. 80-81. Cf. also J. Maritain, *Approches de Dieu* (Paris, Alsatia) pp. 9-24; and H. Paissac, " Preuves de Dieu, " *Lumière et Vie* 14.

or the desire for Happiness—proofs which obviously do not share strict demonstrative strength, i.e. they do not end with the affirmation of a prime Existent, except by the preliminary reduction of the modalities under consideration to being itself. [35]

But being itself is also ascribed to a *subject:* the world. This second term of the initial affirmation can also be taken in different meanings, which are going to determine the different methods of demonstration. All reflection tries to make the world appear as an effect. An effect is recognized as such by its most hidden elements, namely, its composition of essence and existence. This composition, however, can be perceived under different aspects which are more evident, and therefore more immediately accessible. " What indeed is this distinction if not the translation, in abstract terms, of the ontological deficiency revealed in a being by the fact that it changes, that it is only a cause insofar as caused, only a being insofar as it is a possible realized, and that it is neither first in its own order nor last in the order of ends? " [36] The ways which might be fashioned from this proof can be sketched briefly as follows.

1. *Beginning with motion*

The *first way* begins with *motion* in all its forms: mobility, genesis, the general evolution of the world. The sciences formulate many descriptions of this motion: physical, mathematical, biological, historical, each one having value in its own field. Encompassing all these different points of view, philosophical reflection would first of all consider motion as a certain *way of existing*. The fact of being in motion can in a general way be described as the passage from *potency to act*. This passage quite obviously requires a motor cause, for nothing can move and be moved at one and the same time and under the same point of view.

The basic difficulty of the proof, when it seeks to demonstrate the existence of God, consists in correctly interpreting the change of state foreseen in this movement. The idea of cause that one will formulate depends on one's idea of change. If by the word " *act* " (the term of motion) one understands a new *formal state*, this new state is sufficiently explained by natural causes, homogeneous with the effect: *that which* becomes the newborn, the new structure that it acquires, is explained

[35] For the proofs leading to the affirmation of God as true and knowing, good and loving, unique, etc., cf. the pages ahead.

[36] E. Gilson, *op. cit.*, p. 81.

by its parents. These latter account for the determination of development, and in this sense they are the cause. [37]

Every variation in the natural order, however, implies even more profoundly a variation in the existential order, which the former brings to light. If, then, by " act " we understand a new *existential state*, it is clear that motion can no longer be explained by sole recourse to causes of a natural order. This is why parents cannot account for the fact that their child *might be* what he becomes through their joint effort. Their action determines the development but does not create it, and the proof of this lies in the fact that they themselves are totally immersed in that development. The necessity of appealing to a Prime Unmoved Mover is such that, were it otherwise, the world would have no reason for existence (from the point of view of motion). It is actually impossible to be satisfied with causes which move others and are themselves put into motion. If it is the existence of development that causes this, " we encounter an infinite regression, which is absurd. "

True, there is no real necessity to *stop* in a series of homogeneous causes: we know that the idea of an indefinite chain of secondary causes, one prior to the other, at the heart of a perpetual development is not contradictory. But the impossibility of an infinite regression means that it is necessary to leave the order of natural causes, no matter how many there are; for we must explain what they cannot explain: the existence of motion that is due to a lack of being inherent in everything that moves. In terms of the point of departure, we would call such a transcendent cause a Prime Mover, first in being though not in time, but we see that this term is analogical in relation to other motor causes which we experience.

2. Beginning with the notion of efficient cause

The *second way* derives from the notion of efficient cause. It is a fact that everything in this world acts or reacts: no existent is ever encountered which does not produce its effect. At the base of this productive action, we find an active principle, an energy immanent in the subject of action: its form. It is in this form that the immediate cause of the effect is located. But it is quite clear that the subject can act only insofar as it exists. The subject cannot give this existence to itself; otherwise it would precede itself even before it existed, which is impossible, since in order for something to act it must exist. On the other hand, since no subject in this world is identical with its existence, it is clear that the

[37] Cf. above, pages 28 f.

subject receives the first energy at the very beginning of his action from a first cause which accomplishes this in his own being.

3. *Beginning with the notion of contingency*

The *third way* based on contingency can quite easily be reduced to the first argument.

4. *Beginning with the different degrees of perfection*

The *fourth* approach to God builds upon the different degrees of perfection which experience discovers. Nothing is absolutely perfect here below; relativity is an undeniable fact, even in the order of universal values. The quantitatives *more* and *less* appear even in the domain of truth, goodness and beauty, and these degrees are ultimately based on the degrees of being. Instinctively, we understand that the animal *exists more so* than a rock, a man *more so* than an animal, and this is simply a recognition of the fact that there are degrees of participation in the act of being which are quite specifically defined by the very essence of things. To observe that the multiplicity of existents is thus divided according to a scale of values is to admit, at the same time, that they hold a position closer to or further from the Existent *par excellence* in which they participate. It is the absolute term which gives its meaning to every relative existence. Without this absolute, one could not explain why one and the same value could be found more or less diminished in existents of lesser perfection. Everything that exists is judged by its degree of relationship to the Existent *par excellence*, the exemplary cause of every thing that has more or less existence. If one has truly experienced the degrees of perfection in the existential order, then this Absolute must necessarily exist. One can certainly imagine an ideal virtue, which would play its role of exemplarity without actually existing, but one could not learn of the degrees of existence in relationship to an absolute Term that did not or could not actually exist. Thus the affirmation of that which has more or less existence leads us to the affirmation of him who exists absolutely, God.

5. *Finality*

The *fifth way* proceeds from the observation of the fact that every agent acts for an *end or purpose*. Man tends toward that which he proposes for himself; an animal is impelled toward reproduction; the whole world evolves toward a specific direction about which science daily teaches us more and more. Reflection seems to indicate the following necessary and immanent law of all activity: every effort is governed by a purpose.

Otherwise, if any agent would produce a determined effect without being ordained to produce that one and not another, not only would the determination of the effect remain without a reason for existence, but the very release of the action would be incomprehensible. The result of the action is actually explained by the ordination of the agent toward an end which attracts him and prompts him to act. In this sense the purpose or end intended by the agent, whether or not it is known to him, is the cause of the effect.

The end or purpose, however, can play its role in regard to the agent only on condition that the agent actually exists. No subject could act if it did not tend beyond the specific ends which it pursues toward being itself. Thus the realities of this world aspire after the perfection of their own being only by force of their tendency toward more being. This tension, this fundamental order, constitutes their very life and existence. Every essence exists in some kind of order with respect to being, without which they would fall into nothingness. On the other hand whether they are conscious of it or not, they never become identical with being itself. They have never finished existing from the point of view that they do not have their reason for existence in themselves. They are thus unable in the final analysis to account for their position in the order of being itself. This ordination is received from a superior agent who bears within himself the reason for existence and the purpose or end of all things.

Additional reflection will prompt us to posit the existence of an agent acknowledged as an intelligent and free cause. The Pure Act of existence represents the end that all things must seek unceasingly: in this sense the end of the world *actually* exists. But this end will never be reached: the realities of this world are on the march toward it, are already on the way, yet this order will never be realized to the point that objects will become identical with the pure act of existence: in this sense the end of the world does not *really* exist. From the point of view of being, the world is a never completed rough draft, an incomplete symphony. It follows, therefore, that the end of the world exists *intentionally* in the intellect and will of the prime agent. That is the only way of explaining, with reference to our own intellect, how the end of the world can exercise its attraction without really being identical with the things it seems to cause. God is the final cause in the sense that the world is organized and ordained to his very existence, and this order is constantly present to his thought as well as to his love.

Notice that recourse to a transcendent cause in no way denies the causality exercised by different individuals in the natural order. It simply proves that the causality which is exercised in the world would itself be unexplainable, when seen from the vantage point of being, if it were not referred to a primary source, which is God. Thus there takes place a kind of transfer from all forms of causality which we observe in the world to a transcendent Cause, which includes them all. This Cause is unique, just as is the criterion which helps us recognize the ontological deficiency of this world. Each particular demonstration consequently draws its strength from its possible reduction to this basic statement: the world exists, it does not exist of itself (from different points of view), therefore it exists because of God.

5. THE ROLE OF DEMONSTRATION

It now remains to supply more details on the nature of demonstration. It would be well here to point out a frequent error to be avoided. First of all the necessity of resorting to a demonstration is not due to some kind of *absence of God*, as if from the very outset the human mind were deprived of all contact with the very principle of its existence. It would be an error to believe that demonstration has for its purpose the placing of the mind in relationship with God. This contact is taken for granted before any and every demonstration. The relationship of the mind to God is presumed from the very beginning of spiritual existence. Far from positing this relationship, demonstration rather leans upon it: its task is not so much to *place* the mind—or the things it perceives—*into relationship* with God, but rather it is supposed to take note of the existing relationship. Prior to an explicit awareness—to which human reason obligingly agrees—the mind has already found what it seeks, i.e. if by this we understand that the mind, because of its relationship of participation, is and remains in permanent, existential contact with divine being. Divine being as Cause is present to the mind as it is to every other thing with an immediate and intimate presence. If we were to suppose that the human intellect enjoys keen penetration in this matter, it would be able to see what in point of fact remains out of reach and hidden: namely, the existing world (i.e. the-world-existing-in-relationship-with-its-first-cause). The intellect, however, does not possess such penetrating vision: it sees the world existing without seeing that it exists in relationship to God.

Still this relationship does exist, although it is quite well hidden. Furthermore, without recognizing the relationship at first, the intellect senses it just the same, since it realizes that the intelligibility of being does not coincide with that of the world. Now this presentiment is already a great step forward; it entices human reason. If the intellect which enters into relationship with the Cause of this existent is in fact, but unconsciously, in relationship with the Cause of this existent, the existence of God is found implicitly but nevertheless really contained in the major of the syllogism. The entire intelligibility of being is therefore implicitly present in the very first statement. " All cognitive beings also know God implicitly in any object of knowledge. " [38]

This implicit statement gives reasoning its proper direction and what the reasoning really intends to prove is God's existence. Yet we can still foresee a serious difficulty: it can be objected that in the major (such an existent of this world *exists*) and in the conclusion (God *exists*), the meaning of the verb " exist " varies: it is used analogously. If the knowledge of God is implicitly present *in the major*, the relationship of analogy is also implicitly present.

There is no shift from one meaning in the major to another in the conclusion: the analogy is *contained* in a confused manner in the major in the " cause "; it is *manifested* in the minor as the necessity of a cause is demonstrated. It is finally *affirmed* in the conclusion as a really existing cause. In this entire process there is no insinuation of meaning; rather we are dealing with discovery and elucidation in the understanding of being. At the end of the process, being has been reduced to its primary meaning: that which it assumes as a cause in the *Ens primum*.

6. IMPLICIT KNOWLEDGE OF GOD

The solution advanced raises a new problem: how to understand this implicit knowledge of God that underlies the demonstration? We will have to discover what the mind is seeking in this endless investigation. The precise analysis of St. Thomas in his commentary on the *Sentences* [39] will help explain this.

Let us first of all remember that the mind's investigation bears upon a present object. God is in the soul as he is in all things—intimately (I, q. 8, art. 1). If full knowledge would require only the presence of the known to the knowing subject, nothing could obstruct the exercise of this knowledge. But it is here that we must distinguish between different kinds of knowledge. The presence of God in the soul certainly gives rise to an expectation. Basically, it is the desire for happiness. But this desire, insofar as it belongs to the ontological structure of the spirit, is

---

[38] St. Thomas, *De Veritate*, 22, II, ad 1.
[39] *In I Sent.*, 3, 4, 5. Cf. the rather complete commentary given by H. Paissac. " Existence de Dieu et connaissance habituelle, " *Doctor Communis* (1953).

not perceived psychologically from the outset, which only demonstrates
that the ontological presence of God does not necessarily provoke an
actual knowledge.   If by actual knowledge is understood a clear and
distinct knowledge, such that its object would appear with evidence and
clearly distinct from every other object, we must say that the desire for
God does not of itself express such a knowledge.   The simple presence
of God would appear neither clearly nor distinctly.   It is, says St. Thomas,
like the approach of a friend whom one sees coming from afar in a fog,
but who has not as yet been recognized.   The existence of God cannot be
clearly affirmed except at the price of laborious reasoning.   The reason
for this fact is that, even though he is in the soul by his presence, God
does not give himself there as the *object* of knowledge.   Yet in order to
speak of actual knowledge, it would be necessary that God should be
present *ratione objecti*.   And God cannot be an object, because the
subject has not retreated at all nor has he gone aside to distinguish the
presence of God from his own presence to himself.   If all perfect knowledge
requires the presence of an *object in an act*, God is not recognized with
acuity by the sole fact of his presence: there must be an intervention of
a reasoning process.

    In the absence of actual knowledge, however, can we not admit
a kind of knowledge which, although far from being perfect, would
nonetheless deserve the name of knowledge?   It is possible, if it could
at least be admitted that the presence of God to the mind or spirit differs
from his presence to inanimate objects of nature.   The difference would
appear in this: the relationship of the mind or spirit to God is that of
a knowing subject to its future object, and this relationship can be defined
as a relation of knowledge on the condition of carefully specifying the
meaning of this last term.   We can call it knowledge, if by that we
understand nothing more than a union of the known and the knowing
subject: the presence of one to another, in contrast to ignorance understood
as the total absence of the object to be known.   Nevertheless, if the
knowledge of simple presence cannot be identified with the total absence
of knowledge, we must carefully distinguish it from perfect knowledge,
in which the presence of the object is recognized in all its clarity.   To the
mind which falls short of this perfect knowledge, the presence of God is
still neither clear nor evident: there is only a simple contact between the
mind and God, a sort of touch in the night, a simple *intuitus*.   But this
contact established by presence is sufficient for gaining an understanding.
This understanding must not be understood to mean an actual knowledge,
but simply the presence of an intelligible object to an intellect.   This is
how St. Thomas expresses it: " Just as ' to understand ' means nothing

else but intuition, which again is nothing more than the presence of an intelligible object to the intellect in any way whatsoever, thus too does the soul always understand itself and God. " [40] Elsewhere he specifies that this knowledge is not acquired; that it is, so to speak, consubstantial with the mind, [41] that it is for the soul a permanent possession inscribed in its very nature.

St. Thomas calls this knowledge habitual. The word evokes the *habitus* of a sage: his knowledge. The two, however, must carefully be distinguished. In order that the sage be aware of the object of his familiar meditation, it suffices for him to awaken his attention by an effort of the will. No need to acquire a knowledge that he already possesses and is identical with his habitus. But in order that the mind inhabited by God might take actual cognizance of him, habitual knowledge does not suffice; what is needed, at least for the first time, is a progression following the difficult paths of the reasoning process. This is the price of clear and certain knowledge! Prior to the reasoning process, there is no *habitus* in the sense of " idea " of God, whether it be confused or clear; nor in the sense of *species*, nor object. [42]

This habitus is only a simple relation of presence. As for acts, the human intellect in its earthly existence can posit them only with reference to sensible things.

We must now add some specific observations. It is precisely because they identified the *habitus* of God with the scientific habitus that some ontologists, misunderstanding the terms of St. Thomas, drew down upon themselves the condemnation of the Holy Office. [43] The habitus envisaged by St. Thomas is not independent of the memory; it is such that it can never be exercised by itself. But since the word is equivocal, we can understand why the Church does not favor its use. Better to do away with the word and speak of implicit knowledge, or simply of this desire, this openness which is based upon the presence of the soul to its Creator, and which is transformed almost " naturally, " as the Greek Fathers would say, into actual knowledge by reflection upon the things of this world.

Conclusion

It is useless to make a lengthy reflection in order to deduce the theological meaning of the demonstration of God's existence. It is theological

---

[40] *In I Sent*, 3, 4, 5.

[41] *Ibid.*, 3, 5, ad 2.

[42] *De Veritate*, 10, 2, ad 5.

[43] This is evident in Milone who bases himself upon I, 107, 1, in his article " *Ontologisme*, " *DTC*, 1051.

by reason of its purpose: namely, to grasp the meaning of the name of God which he himself has given us: He who is. But it is also theological by reason of its very motion, which explicitly uncovers the religious finality of reason in its search for supreme knowledge. Under the circumstances the religious character of the intellectual search is not drawn from any extrinsic motive, or only from the subjective dispositions of the theologian: it belongs to the very process by which human reason becomes aware of its relation to God, the ultimate truth. The fact that this consciousness is awakened by a reflection upon the existence of things is a sign that things, insofar as they exist, are charged with a sacred character, by which they keep their distance from man and from the ascendency of his technology as well as the comprehension of his reason.

CHAPTER TWO

THE ESSENCE OF GOD

ART. I.   GOD'S ESSENCE IN ITSELF

Go dreveals himself in the simple act of *existence:* he is.   But in order to be understood, Revelation, pure as it may be, must be situated within human experience, no matter how primitive or rough: the anthropomorphisms of the Bible demonstrate this.   Speculative reflection can be exercised only on a created world.   As a result, there is an inevitable comparison of God with the world: God exists, we know him as the cause of the world, but he does not exist as the world exists, i.e. we conceive his existence in a way quite unlike the " worldly way " in which we conceive things.   A certain purification must take place, and we submit revelation to this purification so that we might know *how* God does not exist.

By a series of negations, the mind slowly determines that God is other than that which our experience of things teaches us.   In the first place, he is not subject to *changes* caused by time: God is *unique*, and this is also emphasized in the Bible's very first pages.   What is even more mysterious, slowly but surely one conviction emerges very clearly: not only is God radically other and does not share his nature with any other element or institution, or people or particular person of this world, but even within his very own person there is no *change* or possibility of division.   God is not a composite, he is pure spirit and perfectly *simple*.   To this latter notion (the most obscure but still the most basic) the notions of unity and eternity are also added.   All the details that the following investigation of these different aspects shall contribute will allow us to tell in precisely what way God is totally other than the beings of this world and thus to understand at least what he is not.   The conclusions, however, will not be purely negative.   They are intended to circumscribe the first statement, whose unfathomable richness no negation can impoverish: God exists; he rules over the world because he is its absolute cause.

§ I. God Is Simple: He Is Holy and Perfect

I. THE TEACHING OF FAITH

I. *Sacred Scripture*

It is not very easy to find a clear concept of God's simplicity and immateriality in the Bible.   In the Old Testament at least, the affirmation of a perfectly incorporeal God, pure spirit, is not at all envisaged.   The problem, moreover, is not even posed in these terms.   That must wait for the period of the gospels, when the certitude that " God is spirit " (Jn 4,24) takes on consistency and becomes explicit.   Here and there mention is made of the " spirit of God. "   The expression does not intend to define the divine nature; it rather evokes the intimate presence of God in the created universe.   The spirit establishes a proximity; it is through him that God fills the universe (Wis 17).   Such is the perspective one must take in order to understand what revelation wants to tell us. The fundamental characteristic of *spirit* in Hebrew thought is force, vital power—that breath of air whose deprivation leads to suffocation. Insofar as it is *divine,* spirit is the agent of God's creative activity at work in the world, his force of intervention in the history of Israel, the instrument of his power, beneficent or destructive, salvific or vengeful—in brief, the influx of divine universal action.

The spirit animates everything: it permeates the world.   All flesh has no life except that which the divine *ruah* bestows: " Were he to recall his breath, to draw his breathing back into himself, things of flesh would perish altogether, and man would return to dust " (Job 34,14-15; Ps 104,29-30).   Already the essentially divine characteristic of *ruah* begins to appear: for if God disposes of it at will, granting it or taking it back, this means that the spirit only *passes* through a creature, while it *remains* in a constant manner in God.   In the world it is nothing more than the superabundance of the life of the living God.   It might be considered as synonymous with " divinity " and it is in this sense that the term must be interpreted in the " flesh-spirit " *(sarx-pneuma)* contrast, which does not simply repeat the dualism of body and soul, but enunciates the separation of two orders, the human and divine: " The Egyptian is a man, not a God; his horses are flesh, not spirit " (Is 31,3).

The divine character of *ruah* permits us to say that the life which it bestows infinitely surpasses, in a certain sense, the biological domain in order to attain the supernatural domain.   To be sure, this notion still does not express the immateriality and simplicity of the divine nature. But that makes no difference; these truths are for the moment contained in another more fundamental truth: the appearance of the spirit erupts as the sign and effect of the personal intervention of God in human history. The *ruah* is the element in which God encounters man, and man engages with God in a debate in which " he gambles his life. " This is a dramatic debate, dependent as it is upon the reaction of the divine *ruah* which gives itself, then withdraws, corrects and again withdraws with all the unpredictability of a sovereign liberty having complete control over the emotions that affect passionate beings. Some exegetes have underscored the *sentimentality* of the divine spirit—this incomprehensible attention which God pays to man (be it rejection or acceptance). Human history seems to progress according to the effects of God's emotions upon men. A more considered reflection will show in the following paragraphs how many elements of anthropomorphism such a concept of the divine spirit still retains, but it will only encompass the core of this unequaled truth in even greater secrecy: God is a personal being and by the diffusion of his spirit man enters into vital communion with him; within this communion, man learns to recognize God. There is no question here of speculation on the immateriality of God, and in this regard the New Testament will add no new definitive details. It is rather a question of entering into relationship with a Person, and it will be the task of the New Testament to reveal the entire depth of this mystery.

The sacred writers have expressed the transcendence of God by their vigorous affirmation of his *sanctity*. This favorite theme of the Old Testament allows us to correct any overly human elements that the notion of " spirit " might contain: God is holy (Is 6); he is *the* holy one without an equal (Is 40,25). The association of this title with the name of Yahweh is frequent (Lev 20,3.7; 22,2,32; Is 1,4; 5,29; 10,20; 41,14; 16,20). The simple pronunciation of the name is sufficient to make one holy. It could very well be possible that the revelation of God's holiness is contained in the revelation of his name. " It is possible, moreover, that the specifically Israelite notion of holiness is associated with the name of Yahweh, for nowhere do the essential characteristics of holiness present themselves to us with such precision as in the scene of the burning bush. ... " [1] " Then he said, ' Come no nearer; take off your shoes, for the place on which you a stand is holy ground ' " (Ex 3,5).

The first effect of sanctity is to keep man at a distance—a distance by which the creature becomes aware of his nakedness and impurity (Is 6,5). The root *qdsh*, moreover, very probably means fracture, separation. Yahweh is the great Distinct One, the Inaccessible, the Intangible—

---

[1] E. Jacob, *Theology of the Old Testament* (New York: Harper, 1958) p. 88.

that is the first mark of his sanctity. At the same time another characteristic appears: in the inviolable solitude in which he lives, God retains a reserve of formidable *power*, power which gathers above human beings like a storm, from which a destructive fire can fall down at any moment (Is 10,17). The holy God appears as an all-powerful and mysterious living being, totally foreign to man and nevertheless quite near. That is why any approach to this Being who is both distant and fascinating, terrible and gentle, inspires man with holy terror: " fear and trembling " is what Abraham (Gen 18,27), Moses (Ex 3,6), Isaiah (6,4), Job (42,2-3) and later on even St. Peter experienced in the encounter with power emanating from Christ (Lk 5,9).

Each time that it extends its influence over places, things, days, rites, and persons which it consecrates, the holiness of God seems to indicate a need for separation. Under pain of death no one dares to climb the mountain upon which God descends (Ex 19,12-13); no one will touch the ark of the covenant (2 Sam 6,7); the people whom God reserves for himself are also " set apart " (Lev 21,22; 22,31-38). As for those whom God selects as bearers of his word, most of the time they have to leave family, trade, milieu; they must be uprooted. ...

But the holiness of God does not reveal itself solely under this painful aspect. The distance that it implies is that of necessity, and besides it is not a great distance. The holiness of God is a call: " You shall be holy, for I, the Lord your God, am holy " (Lev 19,2). Sanctity gives of itself; that is its essential strength. It is a force which penetrates everything and fills the universe. A creative being (Is 40,20), it sanctifies all that exists; a redemptive being (Is 41,14), it rests at the foundation of the covenant. And even though the covenant made of the holy people a people set apart, this preference did not imply an exclusion of other people. Under the influence of the prophetic preaching, Israel recognized its " election as a mission, "[2] its being set apart as a call given to other nations: Israel must transmit to the entire earth the will of him to whom everything belongs. The holiness of God is universal. Finally (and this undoubtedly is its most profound characteristic) this holiness leads to moral progress. Not only does it purify (Is 6), but it also transforms: the essential note of holiness is not to be pure or humanly irreproachable; rather it is to do the will of God, to the point of being *holy like him*, by imitation (Lev 19,2.7.20; 21,8; 22,9.31). Transferring the covenant to a moral level, holiness reaches its peak in love, and this love is possible because the holiness of God, without losing anything of its transcendent

---

[2] M. Buber, *Moïse* (Paris, PUF, 1958) p. 128.

character, is humanized or concretized in the person of Christ Jesus:
" Blessed be God the Father of Our Lord Jesus Christ... even as he chose
us in him before the world was made, that we should be holy and spotless
before him " (Eph 1,3-4).

It probably has been noticed how frequently the similarities between
the notions of spirit and holiness dovetail. These two themes are
complementary: the notion of spirit extends from the creative action
immanent in the world as far as the idea of a God existing himself as
spirit, and even as personal spirit. That of sanctity extends from a God
who is transcendent and separated from the world to that of a force which
communicates itself in order to sanctify the entire world.

2. *The teaching of the Fathers*

The Fathers strive to deduce concepts from indications furnished by the
Bible which would permit one to investigate the mystery of God without
fear of committing an error. Although Tertullian scarcely manages to
affirm an existing God without also affirming corporeal substance in him, [3]
the Fathers on the whole are unanimous in saying that there is no
composition in God. God is spirit; he is therefore incorporeal. In regard
to the Stoics, who conceived of spirit as refined matter, the Fathers hold
that spirit (their synonym for divinity) does not communicate itself to
matter. [4] God transcends the sensible. The Fathers are also unanimous
in reacting against a certain kind of pantheism and in this they are simply
following the Judaic tradition. Yet their theological reflection has
realized a deepening that would be sought in vain among the Jews, a
deepening provoked by the necessity of accounting for the central mystery
of their faith: that of the incarnation of the Son of God. Neither the
dogma of three Persons nor that of the Incarnate Word weakened their
faith in the simplicity of God.

The main difficulty with the Incarnation stems precisely from the
fact that one must maintain at the core of personal union an essential
distinction between the creature and the Creator. The affirmations of
the Fathers on this point are perfectly clear: the personal union of the
human and divine natures in Christ must never allow us to forget that
a confusion of these two natures is entirely unthinkable. The hypostatic

---

[3] Tertullian, *Adv. Prax.*, 7, *PL* 2, 167; in regard to the meaning of the word
" *corpus,* " cf. *De Carne Christi*, II, *PL* 2, 774. Much later St. Augustine in his
Confessions tells how he had to free himself of the idea of a corporeal God. Cf. *Conf.*,
III, 7, 12; IV, 16, 29-31.

[4] Tatian, *Adv. Graec.*, 4, 1, *PG* 6, 813. Cf. L. Prestige, *Dieu dans la pensée
patristique* (Paris: Aubier, 1945) pp. 37-38.

union leaves the difference between the human and divine natures intact. In the explanations given by the Fathers, there is some valuable commentary on items which will be considered later under the problem of pantheism.

3. *The doctrine of the Church*

In many instances the simplicity of God will be confirmed by the official declarations of the Church. A twofold concern underlies these declarations: on the one hand, there is an effort to forestall a belief that the divine persons introduce a division into divine nature. There is only one God; the simplicity of God enters into the phrasing of the mystery of the Trinity. On the other hand, there is the concern to maintain the transcendence of God against the errors of pantheism.

In regard to the first point, the Fifteenth Council of Toledo in 688 expressed the common belief in recalling that God is simple to such a degree that his nature, will, and wisdom are one and the same thing (Denz 294). With still greater authority, the Fourth Lateran Council in 1215 took up the doctrine of the simplicity of God and inserted it into its profession of faith: " Three persons indeed, but one essence, substance, or nature absolutely simple. " From this moment on, the doctrine became definitively fixed.

In regard to the second point, the Church had been led since the Middle Ages to reject certain propositions which jeopardized the transcendence of God over the world. This is why the Fourth Lateran Council condemned the error of Amalric de Bene according to whom God would be the form of the world (Denz 433). A little later the Church warned its faithful against certain mystical exaggerations of Master Eckart: it is heretical to think that grace transforms us into God by a " conversion " similar to that of the Eucharistic bread into the body of Christ (Denz 523-524). But we have to wait until the 19th century to witness the solemn condemnation of pantheism in the strict sense of the word. This turn of affairs was an inevitable result of the development of the German philosophical pantheistic systems. Confirming and specifying the condemnations already leveled by the Syllabus, the First Vatican Council formally rejected every doctrine which would allow the supposition that God mingles with the things of this world in order to form one substance, as a form would " mingle " with matter. It is heretical to say that " God and all things possess one and the same substance " (Sess III, cap 1, can 3, Denz 1803). The preceding chapter of the decree casts this light on the canon: " God " must be declared really and essentially distinct from the " world " (Denz 1782). The distinction between God and the world is real: it must not be confused with the logical distinction or the simply virtual distinction. It is essential; the world and God have nothing in common. The distinction is also substantial and should not be construed as modal or accidental. The reason for holding this dogma is always the same: " God is an absolutely simple spiritual substance. " Let us add that the importance of this document is capital: it defines the faith.

Thesis IV. *Deus est omnino simplex atque re et essentia a mundo distinctus* (de fide definita).   God is absolutely simple, and really and essentially distinct from the world *(defined of faith)*.

II. THE UNDERSTANDING OF FAITH

It is the task of theological reflection—taking assurance, of course, from the guarantees given by the Church—to locate the essential truth which is hidden beneath biblical anthropomorphisms. Revelation—at least, such revelation as can be interpreted legitimately in theology—gives us the guiding norm in this research: God is he-who-exists, pure act of existence. If such is his essence and perfection, God is simple. Nothing can be added to an act of perfection. Anything that would be added to it in order to form some kind of composite would only diminish it by determining this act. In reality, all composition is accompanied by an admixture of potency. But God is pure act and cannot admit any potency or composition. Taking this principle as the touchstone, human reason, while keeping an eye on the image of God in its human reflection (how could it do otherwise?) finally corrects this image, and thereby transcends it. Thus by adopting man as the point of comparison, one can successively establish the following propositions: God is *living*, he is more than a body; God is *spirit*, he is more than the human soul; God is *holy*, he transcends every created spirit by the simplicity of his being; God is *Lord*, master of all things, he needs no thing or person.

1. *God is spirit*

If the tendency of primitive man leads him to imagine God as having a bodily form, that is only because the body is an integral part of the human personality. In our experience the body constitutes a central

point of reference—a very intimate one—by which the person is situated
within the extension of the visible world and enters into contact with all
other conscious beings.   Conscious life uses the body as its medium.
Perhaps a very simple reflection will help us dissociate the reality of the
body from that of life.   Our experience teaches us that all bodies do not
live of themselves, and therefore life is not essentially linked to the
corporeal aspect of things.   What essentially derives from the body, on
the contrary, and what constitutes somewhat of a difficulty to life itself
and its prolongation, is extension, for extension connotes the possibility
of discontinuity.   In point of fact, whatever can be divided has extension.
Now the potentiality of being divided into separable parts represents in
itself a basic weakness: viz., that of being placed outside of self and of
becoming something other than the self.   Yet life, at least higher life,
is not divisible; it is a synthesis.   The fact of being extended or divisible
therefore constitutes for the living being a threat of change — or death.
But the living God cannot admit this potentiality of being changed, being
placed outside of self.   He is " too " living, " too " identical with his act
to be extended in extension.   He is neither here nor there, nor is he
measurable; he is not a body, God is spirit.

2.   *God is his essence*

But even here we must clarify and purify our concepts: it is not necessary
to the life of this spirit that he " take on a body " or animate a body, as
is the case with the human person.   Not only is God *not* a body, but he
does not even have one.   He is consequently unaware of the resistances
that the human spirit encounters in its body: this battle in which St. Paul
says that man does what he does not will to, and cannot do what he wills
to do.   But he who is the agent *par excellence* is evidently not subject to
such conflicts.   His action is so pure that it has no need of reckoning with
any instrument or intermediary.   God acts by himself, he does everything
he wishes, he is pure spirit.   No obstacle hinders his projects, no passion
can change or trouble his personality.   The reason for this total absence
of passivity in divine action seems to be that God's being is exempt from
the potentiality of change which affects every existing material being.
A basic property of matter is to create the possibility of numeration, of
multiplication, and this possibility of multiplication is based on the fact
that no existing material thing is strictly identical with its *essence*.   That
many living things of the same species share the same essence or nature
is a sign that each one is its essence in potency or " tendency " and
therefore is material.   But God does not share his essence with any other.
He is his entire essence so that he can truly say: I am what I am,

everything that I am. To admit the contrary would be tantamount to saying that God is not what he is, that he simply tends toward being, as man tends toward his perfection. This would be to admit that God has some potency. But this is impossible. God has no matter; he himself is everything that he is. He is simple.

3. *God is his existence*

The simplicity of God, however, is far above the simplicity of the created spirit. True, the latter cannot undergo decomposition which threatens every material existent because spirit as such includes no matter. It is not its essence in potency, nor does it share its essence with anyone else; one cannot make many other " copies " from it. In itself spirit exhausts its reality; it totalizes its essence like a lord who hoards all of his power. In brief, spirit is what it is with no discernible difference between " that which is " (the existing subject) and " that which it is " (its essence). The essence of a spiritual existent exists only once. Yet if the spirit actualizes all the potentialities of its essence, it does not thereby actualize all the possibilities of being itself. The proof of this is the existence of other spirits besides itself, each one freely actualizing its destiny. That the created spirit might appear alone in its species does not mean that it is the only one in existence. On the contrary, persons confront each other in existence and this is a sign that they are not identical with existence. " For the act of existing as such cannot be diverse. " The diversity which we see in the society of spirits is possible only because of the difference between what one is and what the other is, and this is a recognition of a distinction between existence and existents.

Such a distinction is inadmissible in God. Otherwise God would find himself reduced to simply possessing existence, as do existents of this world. Now possessing existence presupposes a separation between the one who possesses and what he possesses. To have existence is to take one's share of existence, to exist by participation—this means one no longer exists by or of himself, for one cannot be what one possesses, and composition is unavoidable. But it is unthinkable that such composition should affect the first cause. He exercises his causality only on the condition of existing by essence; the existence of a composition between subject and existence in God would disqualify him as a cause. What actually is the meaning of the fact of " having? " It is a certain degradation. He who has is necessarily inferior to him who is. He who " has " finds in his " having " something which is lacking to him, something of which he is deprived. This is the case with a subject in regard to the existence from which he is quite distinct. He is inferior to it. Without existence, essence would be nothing; and when it does exist, it still remains in potency in regard to that which is its act. It tends toward that which confers upon it all of its perfection, but this tendency is never consummated in a total identity. God does not try to exist; *he does exist*, in act. This then is the advantage and disadvantage of saying that his essence is his existence. We therefore must take up again the conclusion that terminated the demonstration of God's existence, and truthfully speaking, we really never left this demonstration. We have placed an equals sign between the fact of being a *composite being* and the fact of being an *effect*. But it is quite clear that God is not caused by an Other, since he is the cause of everything other than himself. The denial of all composition between him who is and his existence is contained in the affirmation of a primary causality.

Our goal is to underscore the simplicity of God. Let us say that God's existence is his essence. He is therefore perfectly simple since nothing can be added to the act of existence. But, you may object, is that not the height of imperfection? Doesn't the expression: " He simply exists, " express a basic poverty in an existent? Do we not say of a pebble, for example, it doesn't think, it perceives nothing, it does not even have the life of a plant, it *simply exists?* Such a simple existence would seem to be the height of poverty; it inspires that nausea to which existentialism constantly refers. This is the undetermined form to which any and every determination can be added. But this quite obviously is not the sense in which God simply exists. He is existence in its plenitude of perfection, and it is not contradictory to express this plenitude by existence itself. It suffices to notice that all the perfection which we see lacking in the pebble can be realized only on the condition of its *existence.* An existent possesses such or such a perfection, including the highest manifestation of life, as for example, understanding, only in the degree to which it exists. From another point of view, existence would appear to be the perfection of all perfection, and it is only by a device of logic that it can be considered in this common idea as bordering quite close to the notion of nothing. But if we take an existential point of view, existence appears over and beyond our concepts as the foundation of all perfection. Whatever is identified with existence itself stands at the summit of perfection. It is in this sense that we say of God: he simply exists, he is not this or that, he exists, pure and simply.

It is undeniably difficult to speak of the simplicity or purity of a being, without seeming to jeopardize its internal richness. Ordinarily language delineates the purity of a being by a method of exclusion. But where the purity of God is under discussion, exclusion must mean a paradoxical reversal of affairs, the inclusion of all values. To say that there is some supreme Existent whose essence strictly coincides with his existence is to affirm the existence of an *Esse purum* without any particular perfections *qua* particular perfections. It is also to affirm a *Being* which concentrates in himself all values, in the measure to which these values heap up in the being whatever perfections they might possess. Simple being, even before it is purified from every defect and imperfection, is nevertheless not *deprived* of perfections that we discover in the existents of this world. The knowledge of the Pure loses all meaning if it is obtained at the end of a dialectic of impoverishment, which would little by little have taken away from the totality of being its diverse and rich aspects in order to retain nothing else but simple and naked being or existence. In fact, such a being could not account for the variations and differences among existents: it would leave even the existence of diversity without an explanation; it would no longer be a " cause. " Pure being or existence has meaning only at the end of a dialectic of accumulation, which sees every perfection included in the *esse subsistens* as in its cause. In created things, being supports all the forms of perfection; in God, being simply subsists. With this expression we show that divine Being has no need of any support in order to exist; it does not abandon its actuality to some subject or matter; it does not dissipate it in exterior activities, nor does it exhaust its existence in any labor, but rather it retains existence totally turned in upon itself, subsistence. God, even though simple, is perfect.

4. *Pantheism*

One more crucial question remains: If God is simple in himself, can it not be asked whether any other being could not enter into composition with him? Can it not be supposed that the world is so joined with him as to constitute one and the same existent? How are the relationships between God and the world to be understood? The question must inevitably arise, for it is a fact that the world is bound to an all-powerful creative force, upon whom it is at every moment totally dependent. Consequently, the nature of this relationship must be determined from all the available evidence. Must the intimacy created by this relationship lead us to think that everything is God, and thus incline us toward pantheism?

First of all, let us reject what is called popular pantheism, which identifies the world with God purely and simply. Such a pantheism is contradictory. It militates against the necessity of recurring to a cause capable of sustaining the universe. If there is a cause of the world, it must necessarily be distinct from its effect.   To deny this distinction amounts to denying the existence of God or refusing to recognize the world in its contingency.   A more intelligent and subtle pantheism, prepared by centuries of Christian reflection on the Incarnation, awaits the philosopher.

Let us also leave aside the more or less anthropomorphic theories which tend to represent God as the soul of the world, or as a kind of primary Substance, of which we see nothing more than the accidental appearances.   Such opinions are incompatible with the simplicity of God as we have just explained it.   The only question which allows investigation is whether God could not be the very existence of the world, since in him essence is identical with existence.   Would such an affirmation contradict what has been said about the simplicity of God?   We must make a distinction here, for the hypothesis is twofold.

Let us suppose that God is the existence of the world, *to the point of limiting him to being no more than that.*   In such a case we must resolutely withdraw the hypothesis as contrary to faith and reason.   It allows in God the imperfection of being the act of a limited existent, and of being nothing more than that.   God is no longer Pure Act, he becomes the act of the world: he is a component part, no longer the first Cause.   But this is absurd: God is not relative to the world.   Not only is he distinct from it, but he is essentially different.   Just as his essence consists in existing, so too is he an individual by the very fact of being subsistent.   It is consequently impossible for him to establish a relationship with some alien nature.   God therefore is not the act of the world in the same sense in which he would be limited by the nature of created things.

On the other hand, let us suppose that God causes this world to exist *without being limited by this universe.*   The hypothesis would then consist in imagining a universe really and essentially distinct from God, but having no act of existence other than the act of God's existence.   In this hypothesis, the world remains unchanged from the point of view of its nature, but it does not have its *esse proprium*, it subsists by the act of God's very own existence.   This means that it is assumed by God or by one of the three Persons.   Yet divine being still remains strictly unchanged.   It is in no way limited by the world, nor is it relative to the world.   It simply causes the universe to exist by its own existence, without being reduced to this role.   In short, could we not think that the " world is God " in the sense in which the contemporaries of Christ would say, under the light of Revelation, " this man is God? "

From the point of view of reason we must answer that the hypothesis is not contradictory, but its possibility surpasses the sphere of demonstration. The crucial question is whether the purity of the divine being would be adversely affected by assuming a created nature. Yet the theology of Christ shows that a real and essential distinction remains between the human and divine natures (this latter being identical with divine existence) when the divine assumes the human. Pure act is undoubtedly *that by which* the human nature exists. Yet in order to exercise this function, it is not necessary that pure act must undergo a *limitation* by some created essence, or that it should be *received* as *form* by a distinct subject. It subsists in itself.

It would be contradictory for divine being to be the act of a created nature as an " intrinsically informing form "; but it would not be contradictory for it to be an " intrinsic term. " Thus the theologian admits that the existence of the Word *terminates* the humanity of Christ, but there is no real relation of the word to the humanity of Christ. (The only real relation is that of the humanity of Christ to the Word.) [5] If the Incarnation could take place once, it is not impossible that it could take place many times. It is not absurd, *per se*, to think that God could assume the totality of the world (III, 3,7; 4,1 and 5; III Sent 1,2,5). [6] The hypothesis, however, is not very convincing; considering only the facts of experience, everything can be explained without this recourse. Let us also remember that there are psychological or moral reasons to weaken this hypothesis. Sinful humanity might not understand this consideration, but arguments of a strictly metaphysical order are even more difficult to grasp.

Truthfully speaking, human reason in this domain has no decisive proofs; and just as it does not receive evidence from being except by mediation of existents—and these latter remain the same in their essence— it is beyond the competence of reason to know whether or not God assumed

[5] Garrigou-Lagrange makes this appropriate observation: " Just as the face-to-face vision of God can be the *terminus* of beatific vision without involving any imperfection whatsoever, so too can the Word made flesh *personally terminate* the humanity of Jesus and possess it without involving any imperfection. If the Word were the informing form, he would be a participated being and would no longer be God; he would be less perfect than the composite of which he is a part. This would be a return to the atheism of Amaury de Bène. But there is no problem if the Word *terminates* only the humanity of Jesus in the order of being like the divine essence *clare visa* terminates beatific vision in the order of intelligibility. (...) The Word is the *intrinsic term of assumed humanity*, but he is *not received* as an informing form in humanity. Neither does the Word *accept humanity* because of some intrinsic passive potency in his nature. " " La possibilité de l'Incarnation sans aucune déviation panthéistique, " *Angelicum* 30 (1953) 337-46.

[6] Cf. A. Valensin, " Panthéisme, " *DAFC*.

the universe. The apostles needed a revelation in order to make a definite pronouncement on the divinity of Christ, for to the eyes of reason, nothing distinguished him from other men. In any case, supposing that God could personally unite himself with the individual nature of all human beings, as the Word has assumed the human nature of Christ, we could still avoid all forms of pantheism, because in this case, the individual human natures would be freely created and freely assumed by God, just as was that of Christ.

From the *point of view of faith*, however, the hypothesis, although not contradictory, must be rejected. In admitting it, one would on the one hand no longer take into account the pre-eminence of Christ over every creature, and the absolutely unique role that he has played in the history of salvation; and on the other hand, one could no longer account for the statements of the First Vatican Council. This latter was not satisfied with simply distinguishing God and the world from the viewpoint of essence. It also distinguished them as two concrete substances, two " things, " to use an inadequate term.

It is impossible to see how one could retain such expressions if God and the world, by sharing one and the same *esse*, formed one and the same existent. Faith specifies here a point that reason, left to itself, could not explain. All we can say is that revelation obliges us not to reject pantheism with arguments that would hinder any coherent explanation of the mystery of Christ.

§ II. God Is One

I. THE TEACHING OF FAITH

1. *The Old Testament*

Monotheism is a basic characteristic of the Jewish religion. It is encountered, though in a vague form sometimes, at the very beginnings of patriarchal history. Even before it was explicitly formulated, monotheism was practiced in everyday life and was expressed in attitudes of trust, adoration, total submission to Someone Unique. In this regard, the God of the patriarchal narratives appeared under some singularly pure traits. No longer do we find in these narratives traces of the polytheism which Abraham's ancestors practiced (Judg 24,2-3; Jud 5,6-9). The God whom the patriarchs adored was ordinarily called *El*, a contemporary and generic designation for divinity among the Semites, or even *Elohim*, a plural form which testifies perhaps to old polytheistic beliefs, but which at this epoch must be interpreted as a majestic plural, or plural of concentration. The patriarchs no longer adored other gods; it would be useless to seek in the Bible mention of a pantheon, or the presence of a goddess consort alongside God. Neither is there any allusion to the birth or creation of God as in the ancient mythologies. On the contrary, it is the world that is born by the action of God, who surpasses his creation to such a degree that he cannot be identified with any of the forces of nature. God is no longer localized in a specific place, as the plurality of worship places might suggest. Nevertheless he describes himself according to his worshipers: the God of Abraham, of Isaac and of Jacob. He is therefore a personal God, Creator, Master and Judge of all, even of men who do not belong to the patriarchal clans. It is true that God prepares a chosen people for himself in Abraham, but he does this of his own free will. This is the God whom Abraham and his descendents have worshiped exclusively, considering, of course, human weakness and the difficulties of their historical situation. It would obviously be too great a conclusion to say that they were aware of all the consequences implied by their faith. Nevertheless, even though we can speak of an evolution of their monotheism, we cannot speak of an evolution toward monotheism.

The unicity of God is thus attached exclusively to the revelation of the name of Yahweh. " I am the Lord your God, who brought you out of the land of Egypt, out of the house of bondage " (Ex 20,2). This bond between the unity of God and the liberation from Egypt is a remarkable illustration of the development of Hebrew thought. It does not proceed by reflection on nature or the world; rather it progresses according to the moment of its historical existence. The question is not to know whether God is ontologically one; according to de Vaux it is " why is the One Yahweh the God of Israel, and why among all the nations of the earth, is Israel his people? " [7] The fact that the God of the Exodus is someone is proved by his personal character, the promises he made, and the Covenant by which he bound himself to Israel as if by bonds of a spiritual marriage. Israel has but one God, one Spouse, and the Divine Jealousy is ever careful lest this bond be broken. But more important is the fact that this Unique-Yahweh, this Jealous God to whom Israel owes its national, singular existence is not one god among many others who fight among themselves for the favors of this people, but rather he is *Unique*. Moses did not hesitate to identify this singular God with the God of his Fathers, the God of Abraham, Isaac and Jacob i.e. with God the Master and Creator of the Universe. God is unique because Yahweh absorbs all divinity in himself: " I am the Lord, and there is no other " (Is 45,18).

---

[7] A. de Vaux, *Bible de Jérusalem*, p. 7.

The unique character of the one God will appear still more clearly in later years, but it has already been strongly foreshadowed.

This allows us to say that the faith of Israel in this epoch by far surpasses the simple unity of worship or monolatry, mostly because monolatry—which is in some respects a certain cultic pluralism—is not accompanied by a doctrinal pluralism. Furthermore, in every instance of its appearance, monolatry could not have the same meaning for Israel that it had for contemporary peoples, for it at least had this distinction: it was an exercise, an application of the Covenant. Conversely, the worship rendered to " other gods " of which Israel showed herself guilty many times in the course of her history would appear, at first glance, less a mark of polytheism than a sin against the Covenant. In point of fact, however, worship for Israel is limited by the reality of the Covenant: it is the oneness of the God of the Covenant which engenders the unity of worship. The people should adore one Saviour and Legislator, Yahweh, identified with the God of the Fathers, the Creator God, and conversely God could not be adored adequately except by the people whose historical destiny he guides (1 Sam 26,19).

Do other gods than Yahweh *exist?* This more abstract question was raised only much later. It will be understood with increasing clarity that the unity of Yahweh is a part of his very nature, but neither his personal character nor his decisive action in the history of men will ever be lost from sight. It will be understood with increasing clarity that the unity of the people of God is not linked with a territory, nor even with a nation, and never will one discover that the supernatural destiny of other peoples surpasses that of Israel (Is 45,15). Even the gospels will not reject the first article of Jewish piety, repeated by generations of believers: " Hear, O Israel: The Lord our God is one Lord " (Dt 6,4).

With the prophets, monotheism attains its highest degree of expression and spreads among all the Jews and their neighbors. The unicity of Yahweh, the God of Israel, is inferred from his universal action upon things and men. He who is called Yahweh commands the forces of nature and even though he is attached quite closely to the country of Israel, he exercises a universal dominion over the entire world (Amos 4,13; 5,8; Is 45,18). This is proof enough that aside from God there is no other Creator-God. He who calls himself Yahweh controls the destiny of all people. He judges small states and great empires (Amos 1—2). He causes them to serve his purposes (Amos 6,11; Is 7,18-19; 10,6; Jer 5,15-17). Even though Israel alone received his promises, the other people have no other Master and Saviour than Yahweh: aside from him no other Saviour-God exists. " Am I not Yahweh? There is no other God besides

me, a God of integrity and a saviour; there is none apart from me. Turn
to me and be saved, all the ends of the earth! For I am God unrivaled."
(Is 45,21-22). At the same time as monotheism assumed a more universal
meaning, a whole new criticism of false gods developed as well. Not
only was their power questioned, but even their very existence was denied
(Jer 2,27; 3,9; 10,1-6; 16,20; Is 40,19-20; 44,9-20). Yahweh is the unique
existent. The arguments invoked in favor of the oneness of Yahweh are,
on the one hand, his universal action upon the world, and on the other,
his lordship over the future, i.e. over the history of men (Is 41,21). If
Yahweh fills all time and space, there quite obviously is no place beside
him for vain idols. Idols are vain because no reality corresponds to what
they are supposed to symbolize; they are nothing but stone and wood,
as the author of the *Book of Consolation* shows. Yahweh alone is the
Master, the only Lord, because he alone is God, and consequently the
only one worthy of being adored by his creatures.

2. *The New Testament*

Testimony in favor of the unity of God abounds in the New Testament.
Christ is the first one to vouch for that, and he thereby aligns himself
with the Old Testament tradition. When Jesus is questioned on the first
commandment, he simply replies by citing the beginning of the prayer,
" *Shema.* " " Hear, O Israel: the Lord our God, the Lord is one. " And
the scribe who posed the original question added: " What you have said is
true: that he is one and there is no other " (Mk 12,29-32). The traditional
affirmation, however, takes on a new importance, unknown in the Old
Testament. On the one hand, it commands an unprecedented profession
of faith: the one God in whom the primitive Church believed is the God
of Our Lord Jesus Christ; no longer is it only the God of Abraham, Isaac
and of Jacob, but the " God and Father of Our Lord Jesus Christ. "
Faith in one God thus develops into faith in one Lord (Jesus), one Baptism,
one Church. On the other hand, the affirmation of the unity of God
demands a spiritual and a moral life renewed by the advent of Christ:
" This is Life eternal: to know you, the one true God and him whom you
have sent, Jesus Christ. " We know that God *is* one, but it is necessary
that each man realize this in a very practical way. " For men to confess
the unique God does not imply merely the confession of a fact, but the
acceptance of a task. ... In consequence it is precisely in the commandment of all-embracing and exclusive love for this one God that monotheism
finds its achievement. " [8]

[8] K. Rahner, *op. cit.*, I, pp. 102-03.

All false gods therefore must be rejected: Mammon, gluttony, idols, cosmic and sociological forces—one God and only one God must be served. In this sense, even when it is a truth admitted by the intellect monotheism still remains a task to be eternally fulfilled in practice.

3. *The teaching of the Fathers*

From this point on, the faith remained unchanged. The Fathers of the Church strove to explain this truth as something definitively established at the core of orthodoxy. When Athanasius tried to provide a rational proof for the unity of God in his *Supplication*, he was dealing with a truth that was already in full possession. [9]   Above all, the Fathers defended the faith against a threefold danger: polytheism, Marcion, and trinitarian heretics. The Fathers proved the stupidity of false gods; [10] in opposition to Marcion and his followers they maintained the unity between God the creator and legislator of the Old Testament and the merciful God of the gospel; [11] and refuting certain distortions of the trinitarian dogma they confessed their faith in the unity of one God in Three Persons. [12]

As for the expression " I believe in one God, " it will be untiringly repeated by the creeds of the Church from the Nicean Council to Vatican II. There is only one God: the Church holds this truth no less vigorously than do the Jews and Moslems.

Thesis V. *Unus est Deus Pater* God the Father of Our Lord Jesus
Domini nostri Jesu Christi et non Christ is one, and there is none
est alius praeter eum (de fide). other than he *(of faith)*.

II. THE UNDERSTANDING OF FAITH

The path to be followed is traced out for us by Scripture. It is through meditation on creation that the prophets had been able to conceive and

---

[9] Athenagoras, *Leg.*, c. 8, *PG* 6.

[10] Ignatius, *Ep. ad Magnesios*, 8, 2, *PG* 5, 669. — Tertullian, *Apol.*, II, *PL* I, 332. — Clement of Alexandria, *Protr.*, 6, *PG* 8, 173. — Origen, *Periarchon*, Prologue, *PG* 11, 117; *Contra Celsum*, I, 23, *PG* 11, 711. — Lactantius, *Instit.*, 3-7, *PL* 6, 112 sq.

[11] Irenaeus, *Adv. Her.*, 2, 30, 9, *PG* 7, 822. — Tertullian, *Adv. Marc.*, I, 3 and 11, *PL* 2, 250 and 298. — Hippolytus Romanus, *Philosophoumena*, 7, 29-31, *PG* 16, 3323-35. — Clement of Alexandria, *Pedag.*, 8, *PG* 8, 326. — Ephrem, *Adv. Haer.*, Sermo 3, 2. — Epiphanius, *Haer.*, 23, 5, sq., *PG* 41, 304 sq.

[12] P. Henry, *Le Mystère de la Trinité*.

even establish the existence of one God. The universal order of creation contained an implicit revelation of the unity of God, because this order could be formed only under the action of one sole cause. Such is the narrow path along which our reflection must course.

1. *The experience of unity*

At the very outset it is necessary to adopt a strongly metaphysical attitude, i.e. unity must be conceived in the order of being. There is no question here of mathematical number. We are concerned with unity as it manifests itself in the existent. It is possible to show that every existent is characterized by the fact of being " one "; lack of being is always caused by a lack of unity. No matter how long it takes for a unity to be actualized, basically " one " exists only because of many existents, and conversely, each existent, insofar as it exists, is one.

This means that *one* is not the *other*, that this tree is not this man nor even that other tree, and consequently each " one " has existence in the degree to which he has unity. Of course, this evidence is not demonstrable, but it can be understood that the *other* as such, as opposed to *one*, is a sign of a lack of being, and that every factor of alienation or splitting or division is a factor of non-being. We do not say a pile of stones is an existent, because a pile of stones has no internal unity; it falls apart too easily. On the other hand a tree is an existent because it holds itself together sufficiently to merit the title of existent. It is furthermore agreed that in the degree to which this " one " gives place to the other, for example, in the measure to which this tree catches fire and is consumed or burned, it loses its existence as tree and becomes something " other. " Similarly, man who undergoes or accepts a splitting of his personality becomes a stranger to himself, he alienates himself: he loses his personality by losing his unity, and to that degree he loses his perfection as existent. Every change, every split then is a cause or factor of non-being: every kingdom divided against itself will perish. Unity thus appears as the law of the existent: every existent manifests itself as *one* existent.

This evidence imposes itself also upon reason as strictly necessary: it is strictly necessary that each existent should be *one* existent, i.e. that it should have reason to exercise the act of being-one. It is necessary that its unity exist by the same token that it itself exists, and this is an absolute necessity, for otherwise this existent would at one and the same time be a specific existent and something other than this existent; it would be and not be. Such a contradiction is impossible: whatever is, is what it is; it is one with itself.

2. *The reason for unity*

Nevertheless, the multiplicity of existents proves that the quality of existent does not exclude every possible " otherness. " From the fact that it exists, each existent is itself in a most incommunicable actuality; on the other hand, it shares with all other existents in the same " reason, " that of *being:* the unity of being is thus at one and the same time the unity of the singular and that of the universal. But how can the universal and the singular align themselves under this same term, " being? " How can we understand that the two meanings of the word " one " meet in the existent? We must now seek in the existent itself the precise reasons for its unity.

First of all, the very *essence* of an existent gives the reason for its unity. What assures a tree unity of existence, in spite of its diverse functions and successive states, is quite obviously its essence. All through the course of its development, the tree changes, evolves, but it does not for all that cease being what it is, a particular kind of tree. Something remains in it which gives unity to its existence: essence is something given to an existent so that it might continue being what it is. We can likewise say that that which constitutes the unity of the human ego, in spite of diverse indications or even contradictions of its existence, is still its essence. No matter what he might do or undergo, man remains man; everything is explained in the long run by his essence. The essence would thus appear to be that by which an existent is *an* existent; it is the reason for its unity.

Thus the manifestation of a unity coincides with the manifestation of an existent. And we believe that the reason for *unity*, as for the existent, is found in the essence of each existent. This last proposition, however, is not self-evident. It even raises some difficulty. Upon closer investigation, in fact, it becomes clear that if essence is the reason for the unity of an existent in the course of its development, it is not the final reason of unity, for essence in itself is *difference*, specific and individual, and therefore is a principle of multiplicity. Experience shows that a thing can be other than its given essence without losing its existence. For example, a thing can be something other than a tree and be essentially different, while still being an existent, e.g. by claiming to be a man. In point of fact, human reason perceives a diversity of existents and explains this diversity by the very essence of things, i.e. by their difference. Essence is the cause of diversity. On the other hand, considering only the pure fact of *existence*, diversity between existents lessens, because *all* things exist: existence is therefore that by which they are *one*, whether considered individually or in common.

3. *Necessity for a unique cause*

Reason has just proven this: on the one hand, there are *existents* which are multiple by the fact of their essential differences; and on the other hand these multiple existents all *exist* by the fact that each and every one exercises an act of " being-one. "   One cannot view this twofold evidence without admitting that each of these existents, by the fact of its essential difference, is not strictly one, according to the degree in which it is distinct from existence or being.   For the same reason, one must conclude that every existent in which essence presents itself as limit and difference is not *one by essence:* this existent is one insofar as it *exists*, it is numbered insofar as it is distinct from others by its *essence*.   By the fact of its essential difference each existent is a happy combination of " same " and " other, " of act and potency: it is a multiple, as Duméry remarks.

And yet this is strange: each existent is *one*, and cannot not be one without losing existence entirely.

On the other hand, no existent that is reproduced or numbered is *one* by essence, since its essence makes it to be different.   It would be an obvious contradiction if the multiplicity of existents were to be one " act " because of their particular essence: diversity of essences cannot be the cause of sharing existence (Cf. St. Thomas, *On the Power of God*, 3,5).

It is thus that we arrive at this astonishing fact: none of the existents of this world has its reason for unity *by its essence*.   Yet in point of fact each one necessarily has its reason for unity, without which it would be nonexistent.   How then explain the common presence of existence in many existents?   And more basically, how does it happen that the existents of this world have a reason for unity?

Only one conclusion is possible.   If the one-multiple, i.e. the existent of this world, has a reason for being-one without, however, being identical by essence with this reason for being-one, this is so because it receives this reason from an Other, or if you will, from one with greater self-identity than itself, which is its cause and in whom it participates.   In order to exercise its role, this Cause must naturally be free from all multiplicity; it must be one by essence.   The only conclusion therefore is that a Cause realizing perfect identity actually exists.   If in spite of their essential diversity all the existents of this world are " one " from the point of view of their actual existence, it is because they draw their " *esse* " not from themselves (for then identity would come from diversity), but from a unique Cause, having perfect self-identity.   And since it is all the same for an existent to be and to be one, as has been evident from the very beginning of this discussion, it is consequently necessary that the One-cause should exist. God therefore exists in most perfect unity.

4. *Unity of God*

Plato had already remarked that one must posit the one before the many, but the condition necessary for the existence of this one is that its essence be strictly identical with its existence. Now whatever fuses with pure act of existence is necessarily unique, for no diversity can have the simple fact of existence as its explanation. God is unique because he is completely absorbed in the simple act of existence. His unity evidently has nothing in common with that of any given species, still less with that of a genus or a potency: on the contrary, it is a unity gained at the peak of actuality. The unity of God is identical with pure substance; it is undetermined perfection, a surplus of actuality that no particular act can exhaust. The fact of subsistent being, however, does not put God on the level of the singular individuals of this world, which realize their perfection only by excluding other possible perfections. Nothing can be lacking to him who is identical with being, the foundation of all perfection. God exists without limit to his existence. He is infinite in act, and it is in this sense that God is one.

We must add that no existent of this world is *one* like him. The most perfect among them only possesses the unity of a composite. Certainly, created spirit is one by the very fact that it exists. It is even unique by the fact that it is the only one of its kind. But its unity does not become perfect identity, since it is joined with being. Its unicity also does not prevent it from becoming part of a society of other spirits with which it enters into a relationship of equal to equal. On the other hand, God is " without equal, " as the Bible never ceases to repeat. He belongs to no society. He alone exists. Everything else depends upon him, but he depends on nothing or no person. He knows the solitude which nearly always surrounds the greatest of personalities. Faith, however, tells us that in his solitude God does not know isolation. He forms a society within himself by the relations which distinguish the Three Persons of the Trinity. Still the revelation of the mystery does not affect the certitude acquired laboriously by reason: these Three constitute one and only one God. God is one. Although reason unaided by revelation cannot sound the depths of the mysteries which flow from this basic dogma, it can at least make the simple statement: God is one. Faith will supply the fuller understanding.

5.   *The meaning of monotheistic faith*

The simple certitude that God is one already demands that man take
a certain position.   It requires from him first of all a *universal respect*.
If there is only one God, everything that is not God depends upon him
and him alone.   His kingship therefore extends over every creature: it is
not attached to any given place, time, race, or class.   It demands to be
recognized everywhere and by all.   In addition, the certitude that God
is one demands the establishment of a hierarchy of values: if there is
only one God, all humanity must be united to the Creator in a spirit of
obedience.   It is forbidden to man to sacrifice now to the god of riches,
now to the god of power, or knowledge, or pleasure.   There are no possible
divisions, no duplicity: a hierarchy is demanded.   It is by ordering his
life and then directing it to the Absolute that man pays homage to God.
Finally, the affirmation of a unique Lord demands that man renounce
all his idols.   If there is only one God, everything beyond him is *relative*.
Nothing or no one else can seek unconditional worship; adoration is due
to God alone.

§ III.   God Is Immutable and Eternal

I.   THE TEACHING OF FAITH

1.   *Sacred Scripture*

The religion of Israel is an essentially historical religion not only in the
sense that it has had, like every other religion, a point of departure from
which it developed; or that it includes a belief in a God who guides or
directs history.   It is historical especially in this sense that each of the
great events of Israelite history gave the people a particular revelation
of God at the same time as the plan of salvation for them foreseen by God,
for the restoration of his kingdom was slowly being actualized.   The
entire history of Israel is geared to the establishment of this kingdom.

A religion which expects its entire fulfillment from history must
necessarily unfold according to a particular representation of divine
" time. "   This time is called " eternity. "   Eternity is that superior
duration in which God finds the power to rule over universal history, to
fix the destiny of his people and in spite of the many failures of this people
to accomplish his designs by remaining faithful to his promises.   The first
character of eternity will therefore be the complete inclusion of the time
of salvation.   This is what the faith of Israel expressed by the affirmation
of an unlimited duration in God.   God exists *before* the beginning, and

he will exist *after* the end of this world. *Before* and *after*, these notions attempt to define the relationship between divine time and time of this world. When applied to God, purely and simply, they have only a negative value. They signify only that he has neither a beginning nor an end. Such time, whose beginning or end cannot be perceived, is expressed in the primitive meaning of the Hebrew word, *olâm*, eternity. God exists without beginning or end, the First and the Last, the Alpha and Omega; he is that in relationship to which everything else begins, and in which everything attains its end (Is 41,4; 44,1; Rev 1,17). Between this before and after, or rather above it all, God lasts eternally: " Before the mountains were brought forth, or ever thou hadst formed the earth and the world, from everlasting to everlasting thou art God. Thou turnest man back to the dust, and sayest, ' Back to what you were, you sons of men! ' To you a thousand years are a single day, a yesterday now over, an hour of the night " (Ps 90,2-4). This last comparison shows that divine duration transcends our time in intensity as well as in extension: a thousand years of this earth do not suffice to fill one of God's days.

This difference in the quality of time also corresponds to an ontological difference between the perishable existence of things and divine immutability: " They (the heavens and earth) will vanish, though you remain, they will all wear out like a garment, like clothes that need changing you will change them; but yourself, you never change, and your years are unending " (Ps 102,27). Even eternity possesses a natural sovereignty over the time of humanity, allowing it to be foreseen and dominated by him who enjoys its incomparable privilege. This conviction becomes so strong for the author of the *Book of Consolation* that it will constitute one of the major proofs for Yahweh's divinity. Because Yahweh reveals the future and disposes of it, he is God without equal; his name implies eternity (Is 43,9-10; 45,21-22). Much later, when Jesus affirms his pre-existence over Abraham (Jn 8,58), his questioners clearly see in this (sacrilegious, to their minds) confession, an assertion of his divinity. But the religion of Israel is not satisfied with this, let us call it " metaphysical, " recognition of the eternity of God. Eternity is not only the quality of an immutable existence; it is also the dimension in which God contemplates his plan of salvation. Ontological immutability further serves as a foundation for the immutability of a will which has freely decided upon this plan. If the believer has hope for a better future in spite of the distress of the present situation, it is because he can rely on the fidelity of his God who remains " the same " both in his existence and in his promise. " Hearken to me, O house of Jacob, all the remnant of

The essence of God

the house of Israel, who have been borne by me from your birth, carried from the womb; even to your old age I am he, and to gray hairs I will carry you. I have made, and I will bear; I will carry and will save " (Is 46,3-4). In this perspective, reflection on time not only gives the believer a revelation about God, but also a revelation of his plans, because history is the very realization of his eternal designs which will be accomplished in a definitive manner in the redemption of all humanity in Jesus Christ.

2. *The teaching of the Fathers*

After the sacred writers, the Fathers are unanimous in testifying in favor of the eternity of God. God exists without beginning or end. The contrary would be absolutely inconceivable: he who stands at the origin of everthing is himself without an origin. Eternity represents in their minds a perfection proper to God. A good number among them see this immediately implied in the affirmation that God is he who is. They interpret this revelation from Exodus as the revelation of his eternity. [13] And they arrive at the same conclusion by meditating on the unity [14] or truth of God. [15] A whole series of conclusions gravitate around this central core. This is why the eternity of the Son is invoked against the Arians to prove his divinity.

On the other hand, whatever has a beginning in time is necessarily created: the temporality of the world constitutes an obvious sign of its dependence upon a creator. Concerning the significance of time and eternity, everyone quite obviously does not measure up to the genius of St. Augustine. Even though all the Fathers grant God a duration without beginning or end, many still remain quite far from the celebrated definition of Boethius who eliminates all idea of succession: " Eternity is the total, simultaneous and perfect possession of life without end. " Let us take note however that the Church itself does not force us to conceive the eternity of God after the definition of Boethius, and that the idea of a succession of instants in God has never yet been explicitly condemned. This can be concluded with certitude almost immediately from the immutability of God, but it is still only a conclusion. The Faith

---

[13] Hilary, *De Trinitate*, I, 5, *PL* 10, 28. — Augustine, *En. in Ps.* 101, 2, 10, *PL* 37, 1311.

[14] Eusebius, *Demonstr. Ev.*, 4, 1, *PG* 22, 251. — Gregory the Great, *Mor.*, 16, 43, 55, *PL* 75, 1147.

[15] Augustine, *De Libero Arbitrio*, 2, 8, 21, *PL* 32, 1252; *De Trinitate*, 12, 14, 23, *PL* 42, 1010. — Gregory the Great, *Hom. in Ev.*, 18, 3, *PL* 76, 1152.

emphasizes the fact that God exists without beginning or end as well as without change. [16]

Thesis VI. *Solus Deus est incom-*   God alone is immutable and eternal
mutabilis et aeternus (de fide).   *(of faith).*

II. THE UNDERSTANDING OF FAITH [17]

1. *Time*

The comprehension of the eternity of God far surpasses human understanding. In order to approach this mystery, it is necessary to begin with the duration in which our existence is plunged, namely time, "the mobile image of immobile eternity." The intuition of time derives from the experience of succession. In the course of the universal unfolding of things, we become aware of time and we willingly compare it to the irreversible flow of a river. The comparison, however, is inaccurate in this sense : that the river actually exists all along its course, while time has no course but the present instant. It is now that time elapses, and it is in the apprehension of the fluency of this present moment that we become aware of *before* and *after*, from which we draw our notion of time. But properly speaking, " before " and " after " have existence only in a mind capable of presently tending toward something that is to come, or recalling what no longer exists: these have meaning only in relation to the present. Only the present instant subsists, and Pascal rightly observes the imprudence of those who, anticipating the future or dreaming of the past, roam about in time which is not ours and give no thought to the time which alone belongs to us. [18]

Even this wandering, however, enlightens us about the fragility of the present time. If it is true of present time that it exists in a duration (and that is what gives it pre-eminence over the past and future), it is no less true of an incomplete existence, since such an existent lacks what it was before and what it will be later. The existent immersed in time actualizes its existence only in a successive manner. It perfects its existence in a succession in which each gain is accompanied by a loss. Whatever undergoes change, by the very fact that it changes, would like to be everything, to exist purely and simply; but dependent upon succession

---

[16] J. M. A. Vacant, *Études théologiques du Concile du Vatican*, I, pp. 186-89.
[17] Cf. J. Mouroux, *The Mystery of Time* (New York: Desclée, 1964).
[18] Pascal *Pensées*, ed. Br. 172.

as it actually is, the object sort of " runs out of " existence; between itself
and perfect existence lies the distance of past and future. That which
exists in time strains to be but never is totally in act. Existence in time
is a simultaneous *existence* and *potency for existence ;* it is not existence pure
and simple. Every temporal existent implies a lack of existence or being.
But it is clear that if temporality expresses the finitude of such an existent,
this existent subsists only because of a prime Cause, and this cause cannot
be subjected to time. Every deficiency ought to be excluded from the
first Cause. God does not have to undergo the necessity of winning his
existence step by step, since he possesses in its fullness that existence
towards which all other existents tend but never actually attain.

God is immutable. Now, if there is no evident succession in him,
that means that the past and future have no meaning for him. His
present is too perfect, too actual, to allow any one to discern a deficiency
which would cause him to be what he is not, or to show that he has ceased
being what he was. Not only does God have no beginning or end, as
faith tells us, but he does not exist in time. It could hardly be otherwise,
since time is a duration in which the existence of one who is in motion
unfolds itself.

2. *Duration*

Does the denial of time lead immediately to the affirmation of eternity?
That is doubtful. One can surpass time and still not attain immediately
to the perfection proper to divine existence. The fact that the human
spirit measures time already presupposes that it itself is located outside
of time. Never could the spirit become aware of the fluency of the
present time, if it were itself totally immersed in the movement of that
which perdures. But the human spirit perceives the unfolding of time
because it operates in reality from a fixed vantage point, which is its own
existence. Its existence is not actually subject to motion. By definition,
the spirit exists for itself, its eruption into the time of others does not
hinder it from being at each instant that which it actually is. From this
point of view, the spirit does not have to expect the perfection of its
existence from another, who would really transform it. Remaining
interiorly within itself, its existence is permanent. It does not entail
a succession that would make of the human spirit something other than
it is; consequently it does not imply the distinction of before and after,
which is so necessary to time. To the degree in which man is spirit, he
does not exist in time. He is without temporal beginning or end, without
succession, he is established in a kind of pure duration. Would this pure
duration, which we sometimes experience on privileged occasions, suffice

to help us understand the eternity of God? Does God possess a duration similar to ours?

Evidently not, and even our most pure spiritual experience needs to be purified in order to be transferred to God. We have said that the spirit is outside of time in the degree to which it takes notice of the permanence of its being. But if self-consciousness excludes every idea of succession, it does not necessarily exclude all *tension* or *tendency*. For spirit is not its own existence; there is a distance, a distinction between its essence and its existence, and the awareness of this distance is precisely what measures the duration of the spirit. This distance in reality sets the stage for some possible events. The spirit seeks to close the distance which separates it from existence itself by the multiplicity of its acts. Each of the acts of understanding and freedom posited by the spirit represents an effort to catch up with its very existence. It spends its existence in trying to fill in this lack of being, and its existence is a continual unfolding or fragmentation into many acts. A certain succession or diversity is consequently discernable. Thus the human spirit has a history that is measured precisely by this duration which is involved in the tension between the spirit's essence and existence.

3. *Eternity*

Such a duration in God is inadmissible. In order even to imagine " divine duration " one would not only have to exclude all possibility of succession but even all plurality, all limitation. God is pure act. Any and every distinction between his essence and existence must be denied and so too therefore every tension allowing an awareness of duration. God does not tend towards existence: he exists. Every spiritual action is identical with his very existence; in fact, there can be no other actions. God is that someone who succeeds in passing his entire existence in one sole act of knowledge and love. There is in him such a possession of life that he transcends all duration. Because God is his very act of existence, there exists in him neither beginning nor end of existence; neither desire for future existence nor regret for past existence; neither tendency toward that which he will not be, nor perfection of that which he is; his eternity is truly " the total, simultaneous, perfect possession of life without end. " This eternity is located above the temporal unfolding of history, but equally above the timeless permanence of natures, or even the timelessness of scientific truths. Because his eternity is no more than a pure act of existence, he who exists eternally also can be called the author of nature and the God of history. [19]

[19] E. Gilson, *The Philosophy of St. Thomas Aquinas*, 5th. ed., p. 143.

ART. II.   GOD'S RELATIONSHIP TO MAN: THE DIVINE NAMES

God speaks to us with words borrowed from human language. We can come to know him by discovering the meaning of these words. Consequently a believer is one who gives assent to the truth these words convey. In such an assent the perfection of knowledge is still not attained, since the substance of faith will one day be the object of immediate evidence independent of all language: the vision of the divine essence is promised to the believer (an investigation of this question will be taken up elsewhere). But here below, faith puts us in possession of a true and certain knowledge of God, knowledge which is given in the language of Revelation. We can call God by name.

A name expresses what the mind conceives as proper to God. This is what is meant by the phrase: " divine names. " Let us leave aside any knowledge provided by religious experience, for these are ineffable experiences. In his obedience to every trial, Abraham had known with a lived experience the fidelity of the divine will in a manner which he undoubtedly had been incapable of expressing, and which no theologian, even a Kierkegaard, could ever explain. But in point of fact, the name poses the problem of *expression*, i.e. of explicit knowledge.

Let us also leave aside images and metaphors and all the anthropomorphisms in which the Bible abounds. Not that these anthropomorphisms are uninteresting; [20] on the contrary, they contain unfathomable riches in their implications. The " jealousy " of God, for example, is a notion that is simple in itself, yet complex in implication, evoking many important truths about God: his unicity, his devouring love, his call and choice of a people. But it is evident that the very concept of jealousy is inapplicable, *properly speaking*, to God. What do we really know, using " knowledge " in the strict sense of the word, of God's essence? That is the question. What is the nature and value of the names which we apply to God?

I.   THE TEACHING OF FAITH

1.   *Sacred Scripture*

Revelation offers some very meager facts on this subject. The question under consideration presupposes a reflective attitude, which the sacred writers totally lacked. When speaking of God, they spontaneously but

[20] F. Michaeli, *op. cit.*, pp. 11-76.

under the influence of inspiration used all the resources of language, all
styles and literary genres. They gave him certain titles: they attributed
special qualities to him as e.g. holy, immutable, all-powerful, and excluded
their opposites. They reserved certain actions to him, like creation,
judgment, knowledge of the future. Finally they called him by a proper
name: Yahweh; but they never considered the potential knowledge
included in these names, although they did take constant care to purify
these terms. In order to understand their attitude, remember that a
name originally was the equivalent of a person, and not a mere representation. To pronounce the name is to attract the presence or at least the
power of the person, [21] just as one attracts the attention of someone in
a crowd by calling his name. Nevertheless, consideration of the value
of notions as subjective products is beyond the scope of this consideration.

2. *The teaching of the Fathers and Doctors of the Church*

Practically speaking, theology first stood on its own feet in this domain
in the era of the Fathers of the Church. It was especially the fourth
century that gave theology its basic organization with the doctrinal battles
of the Cappadocian Fathers, the speculation of St. Augustine, and the
learned theology of Pseudo-Denis. The Middle Ages pursued this task,
yet the Church always remained noncommittal and refrained from making
statements in the matter. Yet theologians feel that some very firm
limitations must be considered: human understanding is incapable of
truly understanding God's essence: *God is incomprehensible.* No name
can adequately express the divine nature: *God is ineffable* (Fourth Lateran
Council, Denz 432; Vatican I, Denz 1782). But he is not " unnamable, "
because as a matter of fact the Church selects certain names to
characterize God with scrupulous care. Few indications, however, are
given regarding their possible signification. They certainly do possess
more than just a simple pragmatic value, as the Church's distrust of
certain recent positions indicates. They do possess an *analogical value,*
which the theologian must spell out (Vat I, Denz 1796). Still we must
always remember, with St. Pius X as he cited the Fourth Lateran Council,
that " between the Creator and the creature there cannot be a likeness
so great that the unlikeness is not greater. " (Motu proprio " Doctoris
Angelici).

[21] P. Van Imschoot, *Theology of the Old Testament*, I (New York: Desclée,
1965) p. 196.

Thesis VII. *Deus est incompre-hensibilis et ineffabilis* (de fide), *sed tamen aliqua nomina significant eum veraciter sed deficienter* (doctrina communis).

God is incomprehensible and ineffable *(of faith)* however, certain names signify him as he truly is, although in a less perfect manner *(common doctrine)*.

II. THE UNDERSTANDING OF FAITH

Even enlightened by faith, the human intellect knows no names that perfectly express God's essence. Yet certain names do have more value than others for expressing what is known about God. The fact that the Church has *preference* for certain words is proof positive of this. Let us however establish a hierarchy of values. By the force of the words themselves, it is more exact to say " God is good, " than to say " God is angry. " We thereby admit that certain names stand out among others by a richness of meaning which is proper to them; they *signify* God, although *imperfectly*.

Imperfection in knowledge flows from the conditions imposed on the human intellect in its present state. He who proceeds in faith does not know God by his essence. He knows him only as he is mirrored in creatures. Even Revelation from which man profits does not escape this law of limitation. Revelation is translated into human words, and these, in spite of their use by God or their later significance, refer first of all to a human, earthly experience. The intelligibility contained in creatures cannot help us know God's essence adequately. There is no common measure between the Cause and effect. Thus it is useless to hope to derive from creatures a name expressing divine nature. Although God is known from the effects of his action, he is not the direct object of " nomination "; therefore, no definition and *a fortiori* no comprehension of God is possible.

1. *The dialectic of knowledge*

Still we speak *about God*. Certain names therefore must be able to designate him. How? That question has different answers. Language in its expressiveness embraces all the steps of knowledge as it progresses toward God: affirmation, denial or negation, finally unification in a synthesis. In the first step, we *affirm* God as a term of relationship in which creatures tend toward him, since it is a fact that our knowledge of God begins with his creatures. This is the kind of relationship that the names *Creator, Lord, Redeemer*, etc., imply. Since these names do not of themselves define anything absolute, we call them *relative names*. Thus when we affirm that God exists we mean that God is the cause of all the existents in this world.

1) *Affirmation*. Still we cannot remain at this level. Certain names are not solely relative. When we say *God is good*, or better yet: *he is an existent*, we do not mean only that his goodness or his existence is the cause of the world, for God would not be a cause if he were nothing more than a cause. To cite St. Thomas, God is not good because he causes goodness, but it is because he *is good* that he diffuses his good deeds or kindness. A proof *a contrario* is provided by the observation that, in a case where names would only have a relative value, they would all have the same aptitude. It would be no less exact to say: God is a man because he caused a man to exist, or a lion because he caused a lion to exist, than to say God exists, because he causes existents. Yet in point of fact we do choose certain terms to the exclusion of others.

And we are correct in so doing. Excluding the word " man " to signify God, for example, and using instead the word " *ens,* " because a man is what he is by essence, while he is not " *ens* " by essence, is a wise choice. Man draws his perfection from participation in a God who can be called " *ens* " *absolutely speaking* since he is such by essence.

2) *Negation*. The statement that certain names signify God's essence substantially and not merely relatively sometimes has to be corrected. Although God *does exist*, he *does not exist* like the existents of this world. An adjustment in our manner of expression is necessary. If by " being " we mean an essence-which-is, i.e. a potency-in-the-act-of-existence, we cannot say that God is a being, since he excludes every deficiency, and potency is a deficiency. In this sense, God is not a being, as Pseudo-Denis pointed out long ago. We can call him " being " in the sense that this word derives from the pure act of being. But with regard to this pure being whom we call God, we must negate every mode of finite existence which would not be identical with existence itself. Authentic knowledge of God cannot be gained in any other way except by negation of all the " things " of our universe. The way of causality therefore also demands the way of negation as its necessary complement—the second step of the dialectic.

3) *Synthesis*. Must we conclude then that the names which we use do not express the absolute, except in a negative manner? In saying, for example, that God exists, do we simply mean that he is *no part* of

that which exists? that he has no essence?   We must be careful to notice
that the purity of God undoubtedly entails an exclusion of the more or
less imperfect perfections of this world in the sense of " superfluous " but
not " totally lacking! "   Essence represents some thing in *being:* it cannot
be suppressed without any appreciable loss.   But God is not a diminished
being, and therefore we must say of him that he is pure act in the sense
that the reality of his essence is not suppressed in him, but rather elevated
to the dignity of act by a kind of purification.   Thus God is not the act
of some potency, nor is he the act of nothing either.   (By this we mean
an act, because of some deficiency, deprived of all determination or
specification.)   He is, so to speak, the act of act.   This is the meaning
of the word *subsistens* in the phrase *esse subsistens*.   The union of these
two words does not form a useless pleonasm; it affirms, as we have said,
that the Divine Being has no need for any foreign support in order to
exist; that it loses none of its energy in causing some subject or some
matter to exist.   On the contrary, the energy is turned back into the
Divine Being by a kind of " reflection. "   That is the meaning of the
expression: being subsists.

Naturally, it is understood that in the expression *esse subsistens*—a
notion which stands at the summit of rational reflection—the distinction
between the two terms is only one of reason.   Human reason, however,
does not stop here.   Considering the concrete origin of our knowledge
repetition is inevitable when one tries to express everything that God is.
We describe existence as we perceive it; and what we perceive first of
all is that " *esse*" is a perfection of an existent, and not a perfection
complete in itself.   That is why it is necessary to specify that in God,
subsistence pertains to existence itself, and not to a distinct essence.
We say that being subsists, at the risk of giving *esse* the appearance of
a subject, or an essence, when it actually constitutes subsistence itself.
This risk, however, is avoided by the very thing that gives rise to it,
namely language.

The identity of essence and existence can be posited only by excluding
from essence all potentiality, and from existence all possibility of inhering
in a distinct subject.   God's essence therefore is affirmed as subsistent
and not as a substratum; existence (*esse*) is affirmed as simple act, and
not as inhering in a subject (*On the Power of God* 1,1).

The conclusions of such reasoning stand out quite clearly: being
subsists.   With this judgment whose formulation is quite similar to that
revealed in Exodus, reason enunciates a threefold truth:

1) It designates the existence or being of God in an *absolute* fashion
insofar as it specifies the basis of the relationship of causality (God freely

grants existence to things by the very fact that he himself exists absolutely);

2) it designates the being of God in a *positive* fashion insofar as it finds in this affirmation something to substantiate the negation of all the things of this world (since God's essence is identical with his existence, it is unlike any other thing in this world);

3) it designates finally the *eminence* of Divine Being. Precisely because God is pure existence, he infinitely exceeds everything that understanding can conceive, since strictly speaking there is no possible conceptual representation of *esse* (existence) (*STh* I, q. 12, a. 2, secundo).

These reflections of the theologian echo the teaching of St. John of the Cross, the great mystic of the dark night: " Everything that understanding can comprehend, imagination construct, and the will taste—all this is very unlike and disproportionate to God. "

2.   *God is incomprehensible yet knowable*

The last step of reason is to recognize that not only is there an infinite amount of things beyond its grasp, but that the Infinite itself is incomprehensible. It is not that God is absurd: since his being as pure being is unlimited, he is infinitely intelligible and therefore comprehensible only by an infinite intellect. Even the vision of God will not be able to remove from our eyes the mystery about God. On the contrary, the closer the Infinite comes to us, the more apparent does our mind's limitation stand out in the face of God's incomprehensibility.

That God is incomprehensible does not however imply that he is unknowable. If the human intellect, as a property of a finite existent, can only comprehend finite existents, it can also judge about their finiteness and therefore recognize their dependence upon a pure act of being. The finiteness of existents is judged by their relationship to existence *(esse)*. Consequently, in the degree to which the human intellect uses sufficient illumination for discerning the *esse* of individual existents and distinguishing them, it will be able to give a name to God (*STh* I, q. 12, a. 4, ad 3). For then, the negations which we use in order to discern *esse* as such will lead to a pure affirmation of being and will not leave us without an answer. Being actually can withstand this crushing weight: the negation of all particular determinations. Not being in itself a determination, *esse* can sustain without weakening the negation of all the finite existents of this world. Thus in spite of the successive negations which the affirmation of existence entails, the positive part of the judgment still remains; it is oriented toward the pure act of being, it attempts to be no more than a simple orientation. God is not this, or that, he is nothing that we can understand—he IS. [22]

3. *God is known by analogous knowledge*

1) *The relationship of creation, the basis for the analogical relationship.* The affirmation of God's existence is possible by the very fact that things *are* in *relationship* with him-who-is. But negation is necessary because the relation is not *mutual:* pure Being outclasses the things which manifest it; no bond links Being with these things, it remains Ab-solute. God exists but not like creatures: the term " exist " in both cases is used analogously. To speak of analogy is to imply relationship; in this case, the relationship exists between the different meanings which the word " *ens* " can take on when it is applied successively to things and then to God. That which lies at the basis of the truth of the analogical relationship is the fact of creation. Under these circumstances, then, analogical knowledge is nothing more than the theory of creation reflected in language.

It is also from the relationship of creation that the analogical knowledge of God derives its specific characteristic. Comparisons with other forms of analogy taken from the order of nature could be multiplied, and these comparisons would still not illuminate the basic problem of being; rather, it is being that gives meaning to the comparisons! The entire doctrine of analogy depends on its one basic underlying principle: that the analogical relationship at the heart of knowledge must be determined by the ontological relationship which it is supposed to express.

2) *Analogy and judgment.* The first consequence of this principle is that there is no *one* notion of " *ens* " that can be attributed both to God

---

[22] The intentionality of judgment naturally excludes the idea that in the proposition " God is " the verb " to be " is used as a copula without any existential meaning. This would be to forget that in the proposition " God is he who is " the copula refers precisely to the very act of being. It is based upon the act of being (cf. St. Thomas, *I Sent.*, 33, 1, 1, ad 1; *Quodlibet*, 12, 1, 1, ad 1). Far from being reduced to a statement of the purely logical order, the judgment " He is " is charged with the greatest existential meaning. It has more ontological meaning than any other possible statement. True, judgment derives its truth from the demonstration which precedes it, but in the degree to which it is a *true* judgment, it deals with being itself, *verum respicit ipsum esse.* The statement " He is " consequently is absolute (not relative) and positive (it is not a pure denial of creatures). It relates the substance of God in an inadequate and oblique manner (*De Potentia*, 7, 5; *STh* I, q. 13, a. 2). This statement signifies the pure act of being without understanding, defining, nor even representing it. That is why it constitutes more than a simple affirmation. It is a name.

and then to created existents without changing its fundamental meaning, as if the qualities of infinity and finiteness do not intrinsically modify the existent itself: certainly, no genus, no common reason can " understand " that which exists by essence and that which exists by participation. [23]

The second consequence is that although there are many meanings of *ens*, they are not all completelv different, since whatever does not exist " of itself " must be understood ɪ relationship to that which does exist " of itself " and must be referred ɪo this being. Still, can any agreement be achieved between these different meanings? Not so long as one refuses to reduce what we understand by " existent " to a single simple essence, definable in one concept. On the conceptual level there is no mean between the univocal and the equivocal. But this opposition disappears if we understand " existent " as a *judgment:* that object whose act is existence *(id cuius actus est esse)*. It then becomes possible to admit an analogy between two affirmations, according to the way in which the subject is related to *esse:* he who exists by essence is uncreated, that which exists by derivation, i.e. whose essence is not identical with its existence, is created. A relationship of relation between the terms compared is thus obtained and some degrees of difference between them is also noted. While one cannot conceive of any degrees in essence (e.g. such an individual is or is not a man; there is no middle ground), one can conceive degrees in existential actuality (this subject is more or less existent). These degrees are explained by the hierarchy of essences, or natures, with which *esse* (existence) is conjoined. That which lies at the basis of analogical unity of these different concepts of being is *esse* (existence), for even though the different determinations which existence takes on in the created world are more or less perfect, they would never denature existence completely. It is from their *esse* that creatures draw perfection and likeness to God. [24]

3) *The aim of judgment.* In forming a concept of the nature of things judgment pays specific attention to their act of existence. This property of seeing being itself, which judgment possesses, is what makes it capable of signifying God, pure act of existence. True, judgment cannot raise itself to the pure experience of act, which would be necessary when considering God. We never think of *esse* without thinking of some *thing* that exists. The inevitable presence of things encumbers our judgments on being. That is why they express divine being only indirectly. But this does not mean that the affirmation of pure being is meaningless.

[23] *STh* I, q. 4, a. 3, ad 3.
[24] *STh* I, q. 4, a. 2-3; *Contra Gentes*, IV, 19.

The formal object of judgment is to seek the existence of things beyond their essence. In order to do this, judgment must be based on the experience of existence which results from reflection upon the act of knowledge. *That by which esse* is known is therefore not a representative concept, but an act or an action stemming from existence and replying to it, because of a complete awareness of the implications of reflection. [25]

St. Thomas says that the affirmation of God at its highest degree of signification contains this perception: we are images of God by our actions. Therefore it is by experiencing acts or our actions that we perceive what is most closely related to the Act *par excellence,* and in this *mediate* sense we know God. That is the only point of departure, for we cannot adequately represent God's essence to ourselves. There is no possible representation of an act or action. Suffering or joy cannot be represented; they must be experienced, or at least things which closely resemble them must be experienced. We have no experience of God in himself. Since we cannot see him face to face nor represent him to ourselves as he is, [26] it remains for us to grasp him indirectly by means of our purest actions, insofar as these actions themselves are indicative of the Act *par excellence.* By striving to discover that element in the act of knowledge which contributes to the meaning of the act of existence and by eliminating from this knowledge everything that could deter us from the supreme goal, we can truly give God a name, and in us this name is a conscious action, an affirmation: he is. This affirmation, writes St. Thomas, " does not signify form, but simply existence itself. Hence since the existence of God is his essence itself which can be said of no other, it is clear that among other names this one specially denominates God, for everything is denominated by its form. " [27]

Let us make quite clear that this affirmation cannot provide us with an intuition of God. It has no meaning or truth except as a conclusion to a reasoning process. Only the existents of this world are the object of immediate experience. True, there no longer is a question of adequate knowledge or a definition, but still the affirmation of God which alludes to him as the Absolute is in no way a less positive knowledge of him.

4) *The other divine names.* All the names which can be reduced to the preceding affirmation will be equally capable of signifying God. Such a criterion is necessary in the choice of these names, since all names that evoke a privation or lack of existence must be rejected: no imperfection

[25] Cf. supra pp. 36 f.
[26] *STh* I, q. 12, a. 2, secundo.
[27] *STh* I, q. 13, a. 11.

can affect the pure act of being. Also to be rejected are the names which necessarily designate a limitation in being or suggest some degradation. Thus the names that express material existence or limitation by species cannot serve to name God.

On the other hand, these following names are to be retained: those which express a) that which exists, b) without matter or limit, c) and the qualities which imply no imperfection—in brief, all the names that can be linked with the pure act of existence. The names therefore signifying the true, the good as such, or even certain essential properties of the spirit, such as the fact of being intelligent, wise, loving, powerful, faithful, just, etc., are applicable to God as suitable terms, because they are reducible to the pure affirmation of being. This is the principle which ought to guide the theologian when he intends to distinguish proper names from the metaphorical ones in the Bible.

It must never be forgotten that the names which we use, even the most meaningful, directly signify what we perceive in creatures. In this regard, they no longer apply to God. But human reason is capable of recognizing that the perfections thus designated are actualized in creatures according to a deficient mode of existence. It is quite correct then to distinguish the intelligible content, the *meaning* expressed by these names, from the *mode of existence* according to which the mind apprehends them. Taking into account only the mode of existence, God is not " spirit " in the sense in which man is " spirit. " But if attention is focused upon the intelligible, essential content evoked by this name, it can then be applied to God in the proper sense. Let us even say that according to its content, the name belongs to God more so than to creatures, but in a mode of existence which completely escapes us. [28]

4. *The importance of analogy for theology*

It has not been our concern in the course of this chapter to treat only of natural analogies, i.e. those whose truth can be established by unaided natural reason. All the perfections which derive immediately from the affirmation of God's existence can be proven by human reason, even though they are actually revealed. Yet aside from these natural analogies, there are revealed analogies which are knowable only by grace: e.g. the affirmation of generation in God and its possible analogy with human generation are accepted only because of a revelation from on high. They are not demonstrable. [29] It will fall to the lot of each treatise to study

---

[28] *STh* I, q. 13, a. 3.
[29] Cf. de Moré-Pontgibaud, *Du fini à l'infini* (Paris: Aubier, 1957) pp. 119 ff.

the value of the analogies suggested by Revelation. But it must be remembered that these natural analogies play a fundamental role in this study.

Certainly the Word of God constitutes the point of departure for all knowledge of faith, and human speculation will not add anything to its content; but Revelation is couched in human language. The words of this language directly signify created realities; they cannot therefore be applied to God without constant effort at purifying them. Yet theological reason has no criterion for accomplishing this work of purification, and it is constantly exposed to anthropomorphisms unless in its usage of concepts it can refer to some fundamental notions capable of naturally signifying divine being in an analogical but nevertheless true manner. This is what justifies the use of philosophy in theology.

Certainly all the human sciences can contribute more or less toward an understanding of revealed mysteries, especially those which interest man. But in those things which concern God, philosophy constitutes the only and necessary means of understanding the revealed data, because it is the only type of reflection—as knowledge of the existent as such—which obliges man to surpass himself, to go beyond his anthropomorphic concepts to the affirmation of the absolute. In this domain it would be illusory to try to intellectualize revelation with the help of other sciences, even the so-called " exact " sciences. Since it is subsistent Being that gives us Revelation, the interpretation of this revealed truth ought to be attempted, even roughly, along the lines of a reduction to subsistent Being. It is therefore in terms of science that first philosophy opens itself to the absolute, that one is forced to accomplish an analysis of the concepts chosen by revelation. The doctrine of analogy thus at one and the same time gives speculative theology both its task and its method.

PART TWO

HE WHO ACTS

INTRODUCTION

Everything that is said about God derives from his name: he is. But a lot remains to be said if we want to know how God exercises the act of existence. Revelation teaches us in this regard a capital truth for the accomplishment of our salvation, namely, that God is not a thing, a scientific hypothesis, an abstract principle, but rather he is Someone: God is a personal being. The encyclical *Humani Generis* specifies that human reason can attain to true and certain knowledge of a unique and *personal* God. The document certainly does not say that God is *a* person, since faith tells us that God is One in Three Persons. But it underlines the personal, i.e. the spiritual character of divine being: God is infinite in intellect and in will. For God to be God, he must act with a spiritual, immanent action. Scripture brings copious evidence to this truth. God acts and his action is not the necessary emanation of an impersonal principle; it is an intelligent and free action. In a word it is a personal action.

In order to discover the essence of the personal life of God, the Bible makes this suggestion: we must rise to God by beginning from the creature that he has created in his image and likeness, i.e. the human person. It is not by investigating the inert things of this world, but by reflecting upon man, the most noble creature available to us, that theological reason will slowly begin to perceive the mystery of the personal God. Conversely, the deepening of this mystery cannot fail to enlighten us about the destiny of man as such, for there is a personal reason why the believer is involved in this investigation which increases the dialogue between God and man.

Surely the development of the investigation was included in the very possibility of affirming the existence of God. To posit the pure act of existence is to say that the highest meaning of being is indistinct from the very existence of God. Being (existence) itself has a meaning, but for whom? To whose gaze does Being reveal itself? An existent has no meaning except for a subject capable of grasping it. If being has meaning only *for man*, it would lose its absolute, transcendent character. And unless we conclude from this that Being *per se* has no meaning, the only acceptable conclusion is to say that the pure act of being has its meaning *for itself*. The affirmation of God is justified only in the degree to which Being is *per se* intelligible because it is intelligible for itself. Human knowledge of God is nothing else but a participation in this absolute and thoroughly complete view. This at least is the question given to the theologian. Does God make an act of knowledge?

CHAPTER ONE

GOD KNOWS

I. THE TEACHING OF FAITH

1. *The Old Testament*

The existence of a personal God is necessarily linked to the faculty of knowing. God knows. On the religious level, this truth is accepted without difficulty even before the philosophers establish it with reason. Still Aristotle, who was the first to clearly affirm a God who thinks, showed himself very discreet concerning the knowledge that God might have of the world. The believer does not hesitate: God knows everything; in particular, there is nothing that happens on earth that he does not know. Such is the truth most often emphasized in the Old Testament. Human existence is lived entirely under God's view: that is the first certitude of the religious consciousness. "For he sees to the ends of the earth, and observes all that lies under heaven" (Job 28,24). This conviction gives Job's misfortune its dramatic dimension. God is he whom nothing escapes: his gaze penetrates even to the bottom of hearts, both just and unjust (Prov 15,11; 16,2; Ps 11,4; 33,15). He uncovers the thoughts of men (Ps 94,1-2), their intentions, their most hidden actions (Ps 139). He even knows in advance everything that they will do: "The word is not even on my tongue, Yahweh, before you know all about it" (Ps 139,4). Knowledge of the future is moreover alleged by the author of the *Book of Consolation* as the very proof of Yahweh's divinity (Is 42,21-29).

The New Testament teaches nothing new: the conviction that God sees the most intimate thoughts of consciences is well established. "Acting in secret" becomes synonymous with "acting in the presence of God." The main characteristic of the Father is to see the secrets of hearts (Mt 6,18): this includes the prayers which are whispered there, the good actions originating there, the most profound intentions. Prayer, trust in providence, and in general all the acts of the religious life presuppose an absolutely perfect divine knowledge. "No created thing can hide from him; everything is uncovered and open to the eyes of the one to whom we must give account of ourselves" (Heb 4,13). This knowledge of God should not be understood in the sense of a knowledge of indifference, as that of a spectator who does not participate, but rather as a concrete knowledge, full of solicitude and foresight, approximating experience: God knows his people as a groom knows his bride. We must go even further: in God, knowledge precedes its object, it creates it; to speak of things or to create them is one and the same thing for God (Is 40,8-26; 44,24-28; 48,13 etc.). The sacred authors present no other reasons for demonstrating the existence of knowledge in God: as the worker knows his work, God knows what he creates, and if he has made knowledge, it is certainly because he himself does not lack this perfection: " He who created the eye, is he unable to see?... Yahweh, the teacher of mankind, knows exactly how men think, how their thoughts are a puff of wind " (Ps 94,9-11).

Nothing has been said so far that would surpass conclusions of a natural theology. But Scripture teaches us something more. Not only does God know, i.e. possess an intellect, but he knows everything that can be known: he has knowledge *(science)* or more exactly, *wisdom (sagesse)*. It is by a long meditation on the notion of wisdom that the sapiential authors, under the influence of revelation, slowly evolve a very original doctrine. This wisdom, which first appears under a very practical aspect, is progressively affirmed as a subsistent reality in God. Then it allows us to see its personal character in order finally that we might discover in the gospel its existence in a Person.

To begin with, God is the author of all good. He is also the author of the experience of things and men, of the art of living, and especially of the knowledge of good and evil and of the moral order, which makes of man a sage. All wisdom comes from God. Indeed God alone is truly wise: compared to human wisdom, always uncertain and partial, the wisdom of God appears unfathomable, inaccessible (Job 28,38-39). Man sees God's wisdom undeniably at work in creation (Prov 8,22-31; Wis 7,22-27; Sir 24,3-6); he acquires it on the one hand by knowledge of the law (Deut 4,5-6; Ps 19,8), but he is powerless in the long run to plumb its depths. The thoughts of God are not our thoughts. His ways are not our ways. That is why Wisdom properly so called is an effusion of the Glory of the Almighty (Wis 7,22-31), an image of his excellence, a breath from the mouth of the Most-High (Sir 24,3). Although it acts in this world, wisdom subsists in God and contains the secrets of God himself. Conceived first of all as a desirable good, but one exterior to God, it slowly but gradually takes on the character of a reality internal to God, to the point of taking on a personal quality. God expresses himself in wisdom as though in his own image.

What is equally remarkable is that in its effort to represent the transcendent character of divine wisdom in relationship to creation, the sapiental movement leaves in the background—at least in the beginning—the great themes of the prophetic tradition: covenant, election, salvation. Yet both currents, sapiential and prophetic, do not totally ignore one another within the Old Testament. Some psalms and Ben Sirach present the law as a manifestation of Wisdom (Ps 1; 119; Sir 24,8 ff). The universality of the creative word is strongly emphasized in the *Book of Consolation;* and on the other hand there is in the sapiential books an attempt to interpret the historical facts (Wis 10 ff) or personages of the Old Testament (Sir 44 ff).

2. The New Testament

The synthesis of these different currents is not accomplished in a definitive manner until the revelation of the Wisdom of God in Jesus Christ. On the one hand the personal character of Wisdom is accented to such a point as to correspond in Jesus to a person distinct from the Father. On the other hand this transcendent and creative Wisdom (Jn 1,3; Col 1,15-20) is incarnate and the key point of history, in human flesh in the line of David. Because Jesus Christ is Wisdom incarnate, it is in him that we find revealed at one and the same time the intimate mystery of God and the " meaning " of his love for the world as well as for human history. The specifically Christian character of knowledge in God is also manifest. That God " knows " means that God expresses himself in a Word (Wisdom) distinct from himself and yet subsisting eternally in him. " No one knows the Son except the Father, just as no one knows the Father except the Son and those to whom the Son chooses to reveal him " (Mt 11,27). Here again is a revelation of God in relationship to that knowledge which God has of himself: the Son who has seen God and the Spirit who sounds the depths of God reveal him to us. This means that God has a plan of wisdom for humanity, which is manifested in Jesus Christ, who by this very fact has become for us, beyond all human comprehension, the wisdom of God, as well as justice, sanctification and redemption (1 Cor 1,30; cf. Eph 1,16). All these mysteries are evidently based on the fact that God has knowledge. This is the only point in which we are presently interested. But we must draw from one word its entire content in order to show the importance of this affirmation in the eyes of a believer: God exercises an act of knowledge. Now we understand why the Church holds so strongly to this truth that it has declared explicitly at the First Vatican Council: God is infinite in intelligence and in will (Denz 1782).

Thesis VIII. *Deus vivus et verus*   God, living and true, is perfect in
est intellectu perfectus: novit se et   intellect.   He knows himself and
omnia quae creavit verbo suo (de   all that he has created by his word
fide).   *(of faith)*.

II.   THE UNDERSTANDING OF FAITH

The task of the theologian consists in showing that by speaking of an
act of knowledge in God, human reason does not employ anthropomorphism, but rather tells exactly what God is.   Since God presents
himself to us as he-who-is, the problem is whether we can possibly reduce
the act of knowledge to the pure act of existence.   Since on the other
hand the unique experience which we have is the consciousness that
reason possesses its own act of thought, the first question is: what does it
mean for a *human* being to *think?*   Beginning from there we would
reason in the following way: the activity of knowing presupposes at its
very outset some immaterial existent; in order to be perfect, such an
existent by nature requires the suppression of all limitation.   Since God
stands at the peak of immateriality and is infinite, we can deduce from
this that he has knowledge.

I.   *The fact of knowledge*

1) *Grasping the other.*   Knowledge as we know it from experience
arises with the possibility of entering into relationship with another.   To
know (Fr. " *co-naître* "), according to Claudel, is to be born with another
in order to enter with him into a new communion of existence.   In order
to signify this new coexistence, we say that a knowing being is characterized by the capacity to *have* in itself someone other than self.   In fact,
only the mind is truly capable of taking something within itself, to
com-prehend another as such.   It is quite correctly said that wood
takes or " catches " fire, but fire is not born with wood, it replaces the
wood—there is no possible communion.

It is also said that the vine captures and takes the heat of the sun,
but this is only in order to produce flower and fruit, not to give birth to
the nature of the sun within itself.   It transforms the sun's heat into its
own life, but does not " know " it.   As for the eye, it takes fire and knows
it, but only by allowing itself to receive an impression, and that is why it
never fully possesses the nature of its object.   The very fact that the eye

can change so frequently is proof positive of this last statement. Man, on the contrary, takes along with himself and comprehends the nature or " reason " of the sun in his mind. After having given birth to it within his mind, man investigates it and holds it up to view, without himself ceasing to be what he is and without changing the known object in any way. He really knows the other as other, while remaining what he is. Knowledge thus realizes a most intimate union in a very obvious diversity: the knowing subject and the known are one, and yet each one remains exactly what it is.

2) *Awareness of self*. One must conclude from this first approach by way of the phenomenon of knowledge, that this latter is defined solely by relationship to another. Certainly as the phenomenologists have noticed, human consciousness is always aware of something " other. " This something, namely, the object which appears, determines the content of knowledge: for example, this is a child that I see and not a stone. Nevertheless, while the object terminates and determines the act of knowledge, it must be noted that knowledge does not become contemplation of its object. If this were so it could no longer be called knowledge *(" co-naissance ")*, and knowledge of the individual object would vanish from consciousness. To be aware of knowing *(connaître)* an object is first of all to know *(savoir)* it, and secondly to know oneself together with it, " *cum-scire*, " to be aware of being conscious of it. Now this awareness of knowing *(connaître)*, even though inseparable in reality from the knowledge of an object, is nevertheless not reducible to the thing known. Consciousness of self is an unnoticed accompaniment of objective knowledge, but it is not itself one object among many other objects. It is rather something like the basis of all objective knowledge. This possibility of *reflection* is the definitive norm that separates spiritual activity from all physical activity.

3) *The approach to existence*. We must go still further. Properly speaking, human knowledge is not defined as self-reflection, since it also goes beyond self towards another; nor as attention to the other, since it is also a turning in upon self. Its object is much wider. If at one and the same time it embraces both the *I* and the *other*, that is because it is defined in relation to the totality of things that exist. Unlike material things, which are self-contained and centered on their identity, the human soul is capable in some way of expanding itself and extending to everything that exists: *anima est quodammodo omnia*. This proves that human knowledge is not defined by any specific existence, whether subject or object; rather, by means of each existent human knowledge sees existence itself (which gives meaning to the totality). It also proves

that, in viewing existence, human knowledge embraces and dominates each of the particular determinations of being.

2. The " reason " for knowing

1) *Immateriality.* Under what condition does the act of knowledge take place? After having briefly described the fact of knowledge, we must now seek the " reason " for it.

The knowing subject is recognized by its capacity to *have* within itself some " other " than self. This power excludes in the knowing subject any possibility of actually *being* other than self. On the other hand, the transformations that are experienced in the development of material substances necessarily involve the disappearance of the antecedent form together with the appearance of the new form; wood becomes fire, but it does not support the presence of fire without being destroyed. It is incapable of actually *having*, because it has the weakness of being able to *really exist* as something different from self. Let us call this possibility of change " matter. " Spirit knows no such risk, for it confronts the existence of another only to assume it into its own existence. In a certain sense, therefore, it too possesses the power to be another intentionally. The actualization of this potency, however, no longer entails a loss of integrity as in the case of material substances. We will say that spiritual activity coincides with the capacity of having, which excludes all materiality, i.e. all possibility of alienation.

2) *Immanence.* Because it is immaterial, the activity of knowledge appears to be a *pure activity*. This means that it perfects the subject and does not presuppose any passivity in him. In order to correctly interpret the act of knowledge, we must actually distinguish it from every operation in which the object, i.e. the term of operation, has a separate existence from the subject itself. The act of knowing has this property, that it does not go outside of the acting subject into another subject distinct from itself, as the heat of fire goes into a cooking pot; it remains in the subject, it is immanent. It is *within himself* that the subject knows the other; *intellectus in actu est intelligibile in actu*, the act by which the other exists in the subject is identical with the act by which the subject knows the other. In gaining this act of knowledge, the subject acts by himself and for himself. It is therefore an act which perfects his existence.

3) *The reciprocal relationship of being and thought.* We have deduced a reciprocal relationship between being and thought; a necessary relationship according to which being gives meaning to thought, and

thought to being. We have already noted that thought projects itself beyond existents toward existence itself as toward its goal. Thought possesses a kind of infinity which confers upon it an extension equal to that of being. We can now add that not only does thought emanate from being as from its principle, but that this is not a phenomenon external to being itself; it is an immanent action of being upon being. From this property of thought we can deduce the following principle: the perfection of the intellect of a given subject is measured by its degree of actual existence (*STh* I, q. 12, a. 3). In an infinite existence, thought at its highest degree would be a pure reflection of being upon being.

3. *Subsistent thought, cause of our thought*

This peak, however, is never attained by human thought. Here we encounter the contingency of human consciousness. Because it is constantly an involved consciousness, situated in and connected with a particular essence, it cannot be a pure reflection of being upon being. It involves a duality between being and knowing that is never completely resolved. True, as has been said, there is a reciprocal and necessary relationship between being and thought in man; yet the fact of thinking is not strictly identical with the fact of existing. A certain tension remains. The reason for this absence of identity lies within the one who thinks and exists: namely, the human subject. This subject is " some thing, " he is not pure existence. Just as the human consciousness is always conscious of some thing and thinks of existence only through the medium of existents, so too are we obliged to admit that man is not pure consciousness, but some thing, a thinking thing, as Descartes would say. Man is a thinking thing and a thought thing, and *for this very reason* his being and knowing is limited.

This amounts to saying that the thinking being cannot find its entire meaning nor its explanation in the human essence. " Intellectuality, even though it pertain to the essence of intellectual nature, is nevertheless not of the reason of essence as essence. " (St. Thomas, *In II Sent.*, d. 16, q. 1, a. 4, ad 6). Even though we have been able to establish that that which does not *exist* by itself must exist by an Other who is called subsistent Being, we must for *the same reason* specify that, with regard to man, any *thinking-being* that does not exist of itself or by essence must exist by an Other, which—in order to be a Cause—must be called subsistent Thought. Although it is true that not only matter, but also the limitation imposed by the essence impede the perfection of existence and knowledge, it is clear that the human subject is a *thinking-being* only because of a supreme Cause that is at one and the same time Pure Being and Pure

Thought. God subsists as pure reflection of being upon being, therefore he knows.

4. *The perfections of divine thought*

Let us specify that in God intellection is inseparable from the act of existing, because his existence is infinite. The result is that this act of intellection possesses all the perfection which we have recognized in the divine *esse*. It is simple, for the divine essence is at one and the same time the subject and object of this intellection. It is eternally in act, because it is not preceded by any state of sleep or potency. It is unique, for it is identical with its infinite and limitless *esse*. Let us also specify that even though the divine intellect differs from the human on all these points, nothing in the analysis of the latter can weaken the conclusion that God is intelligent. The fact that the human intellect is always determined by an object has no bearing on the divine intellect, for no specific object can exhaust or limit an act of thought, even be it human thought. Further, the fact that the act of thought in man is a contingent event supported by a subject also leaves divine thought unaffected, because the fact of *existing in* a subject does not enter into the reason of *Intelligere*, but as we have seen it entails deficiency. Being *per se* therefore is a reflection of self, and we draw this conclusion from the fact that every immaterial subsistent is intelligent, and that it is all the more intelligent to the degree that it subsists in a more perfect manner. In this way the revealed mystery can be explained. Faith teaches us more about what happens in God than philosophy does, but philosophy can at least help us to *posit one fact* with certitude: God knows.

5. *The content of God's knowledge*

By beginning with these facts, we can determine the content of divine knowledge. It is clear first of all that God knows himself. All knowledge results in an identity between the intelligible object and the knowing subject. Since we have posited in God a perfect identity between the act of thinking and the act of being, and since there is no distinction between his existence and his essence, God knows himself by the sole fact that he subsists. The result is that he also knows everything that exists other than himself. For whatever exists aside from God, exists by God, in dependence upon his creative power. Knowing what he can do, God knows everything that comes from his creative power. He has such knowledge of the effects of his power as a workman has of his work. In order to do this, he does not even have to turn away from the contemplation of his own essence, since his efficiency is identical with his being.

God knows what is outside of himself in his very essence or self. He has no need of receiving information from without in order to gain knowledge. It is not things which cause God to see them, rather it is he who causes to exist that which he sees and wills. The world exists by the fact that God knows it. Since there is nothing outside of that which exists, nothing can escape God's gaze. The universal as well as the particular, the contingent and the necessary, the present as well as the future, and in a general way everything which has some relationship with the fact of existence—all this is subject to the knowledge of God. "Everything is naked and uncovered to his eyes." This specification would evidently have no meaning if the necessary identity between being and knowing in God were forgotten.

Still we have no experience of this identity. As soon as we lose sight of the transcendency of divine being, we run into some knotty difficulties. The philosopher asks: how can God penetrate into the secret of my subjectivity without reducing me to the state of a visible thing or an object? But this question forgets that God is "more intimate to me than myself" *(intimior intimo meo)*, as St. Augustine says. He does not see me from without, but from within and in such a way that my thought in the presence of his is not reduced to the status of an object, as would be the case in the presence of another human "I." God is the "other" in this sense that he is more my-*self* than I am, and the categories of the same and the other are thus surpassed.

But we can still question: how can God know the contingent thoughts which will arise tomorrow in my mind? The difficulty stems from the fact that the future contingent has no meaning except for a historical awareness. The future is possible only with regard to my own possibility of knowing; there is no future for God: his act is eternal. It is also in relation to my own power of knowing that such thought is contingent, but God is beyond the contingent and necessary. The fact that the relationship between such thought and my consciousness is known to God does not cause the relationship to cease being contingent. On the contrary, it is God who causes them *to be* contingent. God dominates everything from his view, and his view has the same simplicity as his being.

CHAPTER TWO

GOD WILLS

§ I. God Exists in an Act of Will

I. THE TEACHING OF FAITH

The act of thinking and the act of willing always occur together. Whatever we experience in our spirit is equally true of God. " God is limitless in intellect and will and in every perfection " (Vat I, Sess III, Cap I, Denz 1782). This statement is only a repetition of the oldest of revelations. The divine will is at work from the very first day of creation. God orders that heaven and earth should exist, and they do. He dictates his law to each creature, and it obeys. He commands Abraham to leave his country. He gives Moses a list of his wishes. He rules the daily existence of his people. He gives orders to the prophets. He rules empires. In brief, God manifests his will everywhere and at all times. He wills and he does whatever he wills, according to his good pleasure. His will is omnipotent, and yet it is subject to the will of men, great or small. The drama of salvation is enacted precisely between the will of God and the will of men. The necessary condition for entering into the kingdom is " to do the will of the Father " (Mt 7,21). From the point of view of revelation, it is incontestable that *God wills*. Later on we shall investigate exactly in what the will of God consists, and what are its acts and objectives. There is no dearth of matter in this regard. For the moment let us simply state the fact that God makes an act of will.

Thesis IX. *Deus est voluntate perfectus et liberrimo consilio condidit creaturam* (de fide).

God is perfect in will, and whatever he has created, he has done by an absolutely free act *(of faith)*.

God acts, but since he is intelligent, he acts while knowing the cause. Let us now be more specific: God acts freely. There is consequently a certain sense in which we must speak of a will-act in God.

1.   *Freedom in God*

To act is to communicate one's actuality.   The activity of God, such as we know it by its effects, manifests itself by communication of being. To show that such a communication could be nothing else but a free act would be to show that God has a will.   To become convinced of this, it is sufficient simply to indicate the relationship that joins every effect to its prime Cause.   This relationship is of such a nature that there is no doubt that the Creative Agent acts freely and not by any natural necessity.   Whoever acts by natural necessity is constrained by his very nature to invariably produce the same effect.

As is the agent so will be his effect.   Fire by nature will necessarily produce heat.   A certain tree will necessarily produce a certain fruit according to its species, and nothing else.   If God acted by necessity, he would produce an effect that would always be the same, rigorously similar to his nature.   In fact he *would have* to produce it!   That, however, is impossible.   Not only can God not produce another God—the infinite character of his nature opposes this—but nothing can force him to create the world.   Experience shows that God has produced the multiform existents which surround us, but nothing could force him to produce these effects rather than others, or to produce rather than not to produce. He has perfect freedom of choice.   There is no other way of designating an action which produces an effect freely.   Human freedom is the only possible analogy that allows us to understand the quality of such an action.   To act freely means to dominate at every moment the effect of an action.   Now this is indeed the case with the infinitely actual agent in his relationship to a limited, determined effect.   God therefore acts freely, and that is the sign that he has infinite will.

2.   *The efficacy of divine action*

We must first of all notice the unique quality that characterizes the free action which we have attributed to God.   It is distinct from every other action by its efficacy.   Everybody else's actions involve a basic weakness: they always presuppose certain prerequisite conditions.   The making of a chair presupposes the existence of wood and a worker; the processing of ore presupposes the existence of an ore-bed; the transformation of the world takes place constantly *beginning with* and utilizing the energies of the pre-existent world. For man, to do is to transform. True, man can reflect on this pre-existent material and especially upon himself. He can will himself, and make himself the goal of his actions. He can choose to develop his own person rather than to produce some other product. This self-determination, however, is not total. A human being cannot freely choose to make himself a man or not, in the sense that the fact of being a man entails some obvious limits. In particular, man cannot choose to be this existent or not, because that existence depends on God. Man can neither cause things to exist, nor make himself exist. God alone can do that, since he is the reason of his own existence. His action therefore never presupposes any pre requisite condition, since every condition itself is presupposed as actually existing. It is therefore solely from its own energy that divine action draws its efficacy. It is thus totally efficacious. In receiving their existence from the primary Cause, the things of this world receive from him all that they are, for they depend on being for everything they are.

The immediate consequence of this fact is that nothing can obstruct the efficacy of the first Cause. Supposing that an obstacle might arise, it would be an existent. Now every existent postulates a concurrence of divine action, therefore the obstacle in question would itself be entirely under the leadership of the Divine Cause. Any check on the efficacy of God's activity is therefore inconceivable. God is omnipotent.

3. *The goal of divine action*

God wills the existents of this world with a will free from all constraint. He does not, however, will them without reason. He wills them therefore in view of an end which is his own goodness. This means that the communication of being is not the entire explanation for the existence of a will in God. Properly speaking, the communication of being does not constitute the *ultimate goal* which the divine will proposes for itself. Otherwise, we would have to suppose in God a tendency towards a goal extrinsic to himself. It is the reverse that is true. God is not good because he communicates his goodness, but it is because he is good and loves his own perfection that he freely communicates his goodness. Thus God could not will that which exists outside of himself except by willing himself. Communication of being presupposes an immanent will in God. But while he freely wills whatever exists in relation to his goodness, he necessarily wills his own being and his own goodness. This does not at all mean that something forces him: God is not subject to the attraction of his own goodness, nor does he desire it as if he could

be deprived of it.   He retains his goodness in the pure spontaneity of a
will-to-be that is identical with his very existence.   God wills by the very
fact that he exists.

God wills, but what does he do with his freedom and how can we
describe the act of will in God?   To answer these questions, we must
hearken to revelation: only he can tell us what he wills.

§ II.   God Is Love: He Is Infinitely Good

I.   THE TEACHING OF FAITH

1.   *Saint John's statement: God is love*

No philosopher prior to St. John ever hazarded a similar definition.   But
it is not a definition that this friend of Jesus gives us.   The apostle is
undoubtedly quite aware of the fact that the sole consideration of the
world of nature suffices to prove the existence of a creator whose omnipotence is equaled only by his goodness.   The earliest pages of the Bible
demonstrate that God wills good.   He loves all creatures, as the Book of
Wisdom teaches, for loving and creating are one and the same action for
him: " For had you hated anything, you would not have formed it "
(Wis 11,24).   The psalms also proclaim that all creation is a work of
love (Ps 136,1-9; 145,9).   Actually, if we specifically consider the act by
which God freely grants existence to all things, we can say that God is
love.   A more detailed investigation would also show this to be his
essence.

But St. John's statement goes much further without losing its
primary meaning.   It signifies the act by which God gratuitously calls
us to enter into communion with him and his Son Jesus Christ (1 Jn 1,3).
This event could never have been predicted to us.   No natural necessity
inclined God to take this course of action; no internal necessity on the
part of creatures required it.   History reveals a sovereignly free decision
of love which gave itself without reserve, even allowing a possibility of
being rejected.

2.   *The preparation of the Old Testament*

Many centuries were needed in order to dispose humanity to understand
this event.   The Old Testament is the history of this slow and patient
preparation that slowly leads to the unfolding of God's plan " according
to his purpose which he set forth in Christ as a plan for the fullness of
time " (Eph 1,9-10).   God begins by forming for himself a people which

he had chosen as his own people. Mutual bonds were contracted, a covenant was made; without destroying his transcendence, God made himself closer than any other god; he lived in the midst of his people, fought at their sides, led them as a shepherd leads his flock, and showed on every occasion that he was personally interested in their lot. Then, surprisingly enough, at the very heart of this covenant God manifested some very intimate sentiments: he experienced true affection for his people and manifested every sentiment that a tender and violent love can arouse in the heart of a man. He also felt the ruling love of a Father, and this is the primary meaning of the word *ahab*, which designates the behavior of a superior toward an inferior. [1] He manifested the tender love of a mother: " ' Does a woman forget her baby at the breast, or fail to cherish the son of her womb? ' Yet even if these forget, I will never forget you " (Is 49,15); the passionate love of a spouse: " I have loved you with an everlasting love " (Jer 31,3). It seems as if God were seeking to make of man a partner, in order to establish some very intimate relationship with him. This attitude becomes still more incredible by the fact that God does not lessen his love in the face of Israel's infidelities: he does not cease to pursue his people, like a young man burning with love for his fiancée. Osee and Ezechiel render emphatic testimony in this regard.

The very boldness of the comparisons, however, leads us to wonder whether we are dealing with real relationships or only simple *images*. God remains the Lord who has nothing in common with the littleness of his creatures. In his goodness, mercy, and tenderness, does God really intend to surpass the relationship of a loving Master with his servant, and does he really want to introduce this servant into the intimacy of his personal life? Furthermore, what do we really expect in the future: the definitive establishment of the kingdom of God over the world? Or should we expect more than that? And if God calls men to share in his life, how can we conceive a personal and total community? To all these questions the Old Testament was incapable of giving a satisfactory answer: we had to await the revelation of God's plan in Jesus Christ. [2]

3. *New Testament Doctrine*

1) The doctrine of the New Testament is determined by that capital event, the Incarnation. The apparition of the Son in this world is identical with the " epiphany " of love as it exists in God. It expresses not only

---

[1] E. Jacob, *op. cit.*, p. 108.
[2] K. Rahner, *op. cit.*, I, pp. 88-89; 118-19.

the fact but also the content of this love. Jesus actually appears as the
" beloved " par excellence (Mt 3,17; 17,15), the object of the Father's
good pleasure, the " Son of his charity " (Col 1,13). Only the Incarnation
could teach us this hitherto unfathomable fact: the Father loves the Son,
and the Son loves the Father and as a consequence not only is Love in
God, but " God is Love " (1 Jn 4,16), being at one and the same time
both the subject and object of his own love. In this sense the New
Testament gives us a revelation unknown to the prophets: God is a
communion of the Father, Son and Spirit. He is " he who loves "
absolutely—that is his essence; that is the new name which " he who is "
assumed. The definition of *agape* then must begin with God.

2) The Incarnation is not only a revelation of the love which the
Father has for his son, but it is also the revelation of the love that God
has for the world. That is the immediate meaning of the phrase " God
is love ": it means that " Yes, God loved the world so much that he gave
his only Son, so that everyone who believes in him may not be lost but
may have eternal life " (Jn 3,16). A lasting, irrevocable gift, by which
the Son, in sharing our nature, gives us the power to become *children of
God* (Jn 1,12). This is the event that dominates all time and fulfills it.
" Think of the love the Father has lavished on us, by letting us be called
children of God; and that is what we are " (1 Jn 3,1). St. Paul is even
more specific: " They are the ones he chose specially long ago and intended
to become true images of his Son, so that his Son might be the eldest of
many brothers " (Rom 8,29). This sonship, by which the Christian shares
in the Son's filiation by nature, constitutes the first effect of the Love
which God bears toward us. That divine love is the reason for the love
which we give to him: " For love comes from God, and everyone who loves
is begotten by God and knows God " (1 Jn 4,7). The resultant familial
community thus makes it possible for man to enter into communion
with the Father and the Son. Incorporated into and assimilated with
the Son, Christians, themselves adopted sons, are *objects of the Father's
love, ēgapeménoi* (1 Thess 1,4; 2 Thess 2,13; Rom 8,39; Eph 2,4; Col 3,12),
as well as objects of the *Son's love*. The Son loves us with a love like
unto the love that the Father has for him (Jn 15,19). God created a
communion that already exists in him. "Therefore what he seeks and
creates between himself and us, which follows the pattern of the
communion between himself and us, is in fact nothing else but what he
wills and completes and therefore is in himself. It therefore follows that
as he receives us through his Son into his fellowship with himself, this is
the one necessity, salvation, and blessing for us, than which there is no
greater blessing—no greater because God has nothing higher than this

to give, namely himself; because in giving us himself he has given us every blessing. We recognize and appreciate this blessing when we describe God's being more specifically in the statement that he is the One who loves. That he is God—the Godhead of God—consists in the fact that he loves, and it is the expression of his loving that he seeks and creates fellowship with us. " [3]

3) The love by which God engenders new life in us does not leave the Christian passive under the action of grace. On the contrary, the love of God provokes him to act with a similar action of love. In fact, God creates this *action*. " But any man who loves God is known by him " (1 Cor 8,3), i.e. created by him in this specific perfection. By some kind of overpowering logic, this similarity of nature of itself leads to an imitation of these actions. *Agape* thus is the expression of the nature of the Christian, just as it is the expression of divine nature. " Try, then, to imitate God, as children of his that he loves, and follow Christ by loving as he loved you, giving himself up in our place as a fragrant offering and a sacrifice to God " (Eph 5,1-2), St. Paul rightly concludes. St. John speaks in still clearer terms: " We are to love, then, because he loved us first " (1 Jn 4,19). It is in sonship by grace that the new commandment has its roots: love one another.

It is known that the originality of the New Testament consists precisely in the fact that the second commandment is *like unto* the first, because the love of neighbor itself is *similar* to the love with which Christ has loved us and with which he is loved by his Father. This is the " newness " brought by Christ: " I give you a new commandment: love one another; just as I have loved you, you also must love one another " (Jn 13,34; cf. 13,14; 15,4-9; 15,22-27; 17,21; 17,23). If grace had not actualized a common life between God and man, love for God would be reduced to respectful adoration from which our neighbor could never benefit, since worship is reserved to God alone. The similarity of the two commandments therefore can be understood only by this common life engendered by grace. Grace allows the Christian to love his brother with the same kind of love with which God loves himself and loves us. Now we can understand the superiority of charity over the observances of the law and even over worship (Mt 5,24; Mk 12,33; Lk 11,42). The love which God bears toward us results in a communion which has no other reason for existence than itself. It alone becomes the reason and principle of all the activities of man, especially his total consecration to the service

---

[3] K. Barth, *Church Dogmatics*, II, 1, tr. by T. H. L. Parker and others (Edinburgh: T. & T. Clark, 1957) p. 275.

of God and the human community. Everything must be impregnated with this love which God has planted in our hearts by his Spirit (Rom 5,5; Gal 4,6; 1 Jn 3,24; 4,13).

4) " Communion " with God evidently remains a mystery, but there is one fact that undeniably reveals the love of the Father to anyone who might still doubt its existence: he did not hesitate to sacrifice his natural Son in order to assure his adopted sons of their eternal happiness. " But what proves that God loves us is that Christ died for us while we were still sinners " (Rom 5,7-8; cf. Eph 2,9; Mk 12,26). The love of the *Father of mercies* is the reason for our salvation (2 Cor 1,3). The communion restored by God retroactively confirms the opposition between the Creator and the creature, the thrice holy God and the unwitting sinner. The Christian is, so to speak, doubly saved. Not only is he called to live in intimacy with God, but he is snatched away by a totally gratuitous mercy from death which was the wages of sin, so much so that sin itself, by its effacement becomes the clearest sign of divine love. *Felix culpa...* Such is the conviction of the Christian who can repeat after St. Paul: " I live by faith in Christ who has loved me and given himself for me. " There again the Christian must not remain passive under the action of this grace of mercy; he is invited and impelled to show mercy similar to that of the heavenly Father (Col 3,12-14); to become perfect like him in exercising charity to the point of loving one's enemies (Mt 5,43-48; Lk 6,26-35); to sacrifice one's strength for one's brothers in strict imitation of Christ: " And follow Christ by loving as he loved you, giving himself up in our place... " (Eph 5,1-2; 5,25).

5) Nothing characterizes the *priority* of the love of God better than his mercy toward sinners. Love has created us; an absolutely gratuitous act of divine free will has chosen and redeemed us. In everything God has loved us first, by a choice that gives rise to reciprocity. " You did not choose me, no I chose you... " (Jn 15,16). He is merciful to whomever he pleases, so that no one can glory before him. He loves whom he wills independently of the qualities of the objects of his delight. With a sovereign freedom, God transforms vessels of anger into vessels of mercy: no law forces him, no practice of the law can free him in regard to his gifts. This is how the justice of God operates. He himself gives the things he seeks in return, for he is at the beginning of every good and all perfection. [4]

---

[4] Cf. C. Spicq, *Agapé*, for an exhaustive and well documented analysis of all the New Testament texts.

Thesis X. *Deus charitas est: in hoc cognovimus charitatem Dei quoniam Pater misit Filium suum salvatorem mundi ut nos, renati in Filio, diligamus qui prior dilexit nos.*

God is love. We have known the love of God in that God has sent his Son as Saviour of the world so that we ourselves, reborn in the Son, would be able to love him who has loved us first.

II. THE UNDERSTANDING OF FAITH

1. *God is love*

The love of God is an abyss of mystery, which the Cross of Christ has rendered still more impenetrable. Theological reason will never fully be able to explain it. Still it should try to gain a fuller understanding by examining the experiences at its disposal. It was through such experiences that the Apostles learned about the love of Christ, and Christ himself did not avoid using analogies of human love. But that is precisely the question: is there any analogy?

In order to show the analogy, we shall take human love in its widest sense. We will leave aside the supernatural character of the human love of charity (this will be treated later), for charity itself cannot be understood theologically without reference to natural love, the only love immediately accessible to us.

1) *The analogy from human love.* Generally speaking, love is an *impulse toward good:* he who loves seeks the good in order to achieve satisfaction in it. By its very object, therefore, love is a primary and fundamental tendency: all the other movements of the appetite are related to it or presuppose it. Shame is detestation of evil when the latter is opposed to the good which is loved. Sorrow is aroused by the absence of good which is loved. Joy presupposes the presence of good; desire, the possibility of attaining it, etc. Love is present in each case.

The tendency toward good is so basic that it is found even in the lowest existents in the degree to which one finds in them a kind of ruling instinct that impels them to increase, defend and conserve their being. To tend toward being or good is one and the same thing, since being perfects everything that exists. If then we call this primary instinct of being love, love is found in everything that exists. Yet that which makes the sensible appetite superior to the simple, brute appetite found in nonliving things, is precisely the fact that it tends toward a good large enough to allow *communion* with any " other " that pursues this same good. The plant grows only towards *its* own good, to which no other can aspire. The good which attracts it allows it to exist only within the limits of its nature. But knowledge, by the increase that it procures, opens a field of existence in which the affective tendency, while never ceasing to be pleased in itself, finds a possibility of being pleased in an *other*. It thus delineates the terrain of com-placence, i.e. of co-existence in good. Wherever the common good appears, *reciprocity* becomes desirable. Those who are in love appreciate togetherness. Consider the child in the arms of its mother; each one is sensitive to the other in a very immediate kind of togetherness. Yet precisely because it is concretized in organic passions, sensible love runs into certain limitations, the limitations of flesh which characterize the common good. The fusion between lovers on this level is never perfect: an unbridgeable exteriority always remains.

Then a twofold risk can result. On the one hand, the lover is carried away by desire, devoured by his passion. In this transport he is so taken up with his object that he forgets himself, falls into ecstacy, and loses sight of the common good. Or the lover is overly taken up with himself. His joy is so strong that he becomes enervated in his pleasure, neglecting the good of the other to the point of forgetting the common good which has left him far behind. This danger of extroversion and introversion is inherent in all sensible affectivity, and equivocation is always a possibility. The act of receiving might not correspond to the act of giving and the fusion might never be achieved, because the common good pursued is too narrow to give way to a true coexistence.

Does such a love exist in which it would be possible to give of oneself without losing oneself and possessing another without destroying him? Yes, and it is spiritual love. Man gives the other the right of freely using him without, for all that, losing his self-autonomy. The permanent possession of self warrants the permanent gift of self. Perfect reciprocity, even in the most intimate gift, becomes possible because intellectual knowledge which is at the basis of love regards the other as such. It is no longer the superficial beauty of another, or his interesting qualities that I notice, so as to make them the goal of my actions; rather it is his very individuality. Love goes straight to the person; I know the other as another self. That which I give him is not just some thing, or a simple pleasure; both of us together, he and I, give to one another. In short, I wish him good, an increase of existence. In this measure love arises as a result of existence; I love in order " *to be* (given to) an other, " and I offer him the occasion " *to be* (enriched by) me. " It is an act which has

no other finality but *being* and which is its own reward, fully good.
The reason for this perfection is that the intellect, in relating to being
itself, discovers *the* good as such, i.e. the good whose extension is universal,
because it embraces everything that exists.   This good is the basis for
the most complete communion possible.   Since *being* becomes the very
reason of love, I can coexist with the other in a most perfect fashion in
precisely the degree to which we both *exist*.   But we must decidedly
surpass the order of sensible passions, for these latter relate to being
only in an accidental way.   Only spiritual love has the same extension
as being.

2) *Love in God*.   At this point we have reached the height of love
if experience has not led us to some deceiving conclusions.   For there is
a certain distance between him whom I love (a specific person) and the
reason why I love him (being itself), and also between the act of loving
by which I-exist-for-him and he-for-me and the act by which we are one
and an other.   Good is not identical with the immediate object of love.
Good is pursued only through the medium of an other; it is through this
other and myself in the presence of this other that good slowly takes on
the appearance of being beneficent *(diffusivum)* and attractive *(deside-
ratum)*.   Nevertheless, the level of love that man experiences within
himself is not to be confused with the primary energy of its source.
If in communion with another I pursue the perfection of being, neither he
nor I are identical with that which constitutes the common reason of
our love: existence itself.   The otherness which irremediably separates
us—*our essence*—prevents the total fusion of our lives.

Yet is it not the dream of those who tend toward good to put all
that they are into the very act of loving?   To spend one's life in loving?
In God this dream is a reality, the identity is perfect; in him there is no
difference between the lover, the reason for loving, and the loved one,
since God's will is identical with his being, and being is identical with the
Supreme Good.   Since his will is at one and the same time the subject
and object of his love, it grasps being in such a way that we can not only
say that God loves, but that he is love.   His love, moreover, is the full
possession of its object.   He knows no lust nor transport; no hatred,
since in God everything is love; no sadness, since his love rejoices in
present good; no desire, because his love rests in his very existence.
That which makes God to be God is the pure act of loving, and this act
is his very being.   "Once again," writes E. Gilson, "natural theology
and revealed theology find common ground on the level of existence." [5]

---

[5] E. Gilson, *The Christian Philosophy of St. Thomas Aquinas*, 5th ed., p. 118.

Of itself human reason undoubtedly does not know that love in God is the communion of Three Persons. But if the content of this love is beyond the ken of human reason, its existence is certainly not hidden from it, and this is the imperfect manner in which reason draws its understanding of faith. When faith tells us that God is love, this term should be applied to him properly, not just metaphorically; we can truly affirm this from the analogy with human love in its spiritual form.

2. *Disinterestedness of the Creator*

The fullness that God experiences in the love of his own good in no way hinders him from loving things other than himself, for all particular goods are included in the love of the ultimate good. In this regard, no stronger or more unselfish love could be imagined than divine love. If love consists in willing good to those who are loved, God loves everything that exists since his will causes the very existence of things. Furthermore, the act by which things exist is the same act by which they are also good. Divine love thus surpasses in generosity everything that we can experience on our level. Ordinarily, things or persons attract us by their beauty; their goodness inclines us to love them and no matter what kind of good we bring them, we are still dealing with a subject that existed prior to our interest in it. But nothing exists prior to the love of God, nothing incites him or seduces him, since it is he who by his creative obligingness infuses goodness into things by conferring existence upon them. In granting his gifts, God creates the subject who receives them. Everything depends upon God's love: every good, all spiritual growth, every movement of the heart and mind. It is in this creative sense that we must understand that God loves us first. This is why there can be no restlessness, no more illusions; there remains only overwhelming certitude: I am loved inasmuch as and so much as I *exist*. It is not sufficient to exist only to be loved by men; my existence is evidence of God's love. God does not love us because we are good or just; he loves us because he loves us—he gives himself to us by giving us *existence for his sake in justice* and holiness. In a word, the Bible tells us that God loves us by reason of his own goodness, because of his name, because he is " he who loves " (Ps 79,9; 106,8; Is 41,21; Jer 14,21). No selfish move impels him. God knows no need; he freely communicates whatever he possesses. Neither is he guilty of *egoism:* egoism would consist in "taking advantage of " or "using" a person by ignoring the integrity of his personality. In granting us existence itself, God united his most intimate core with our most intimate core: " drawing us to himself, " he called our personal and free being into existence. This is because God's love is not based on passion, or self-interest, or even on the genius or sanctity of the human order, but upon the pure Act of goodness which is identical with his love.

3. *Divine preferences*

Considered in itself, God's love knows neither heights nor depths, nor can its intensity ever be lessened. This does not mean that he loves all things equally from the viewpoint of the *effect* of his love. If he freely grants to each thing the degree of goodness that constitutes its perfection, it is only because he wills that degree more than any other, and since every " greater " has divine love for its cause, we can say, from the viewpoint of created things, that God loves one more than the other. Still, the preference that he shows toward some involves no harm to others. Aside from the fact that beings mutually complement each other by their diversity, God strictly speaking does not prefer one individual to *another*. He does, however, prefer each individual to the *nothingness* from which he has drawn him, and each of the elect to the sinner he once was. Everything—even the most hardened infidel—is the object of all the love it can receive, since its very existence presupposes an infinite love. This is the sense in which God *prefers:* yet he has no favorites.

Among all existents, God especially seems to have singled out spiritual creatures. By the very fact that they possess consciousness, such creatures recognize the Love which has created them. This recognition becomes still more clear in the experience of reciprocal love called *friendship*, the grace which God has given them in Christ. Irrational creatures cannot enjoy the love of friendship, as St. Thomas explains. " Friendship cannot exist except towards rational creatures, who are capable of returning love, and communicating one with another in the various works of life, and who may fare well or ill, according to the changes of fortune or happiness; even as to them is benevolence properly speaking exercised; but irrational creatures cannot attain to loving God, nor to any share in the intellectual and beatific life that he lives. Strictly speaking, therefore, God does not love irrational creatures with the love of friendship, but as it were with the love of desire, insofar as he orders them to rational creatures, and even to himself. Yet this is not because he stands in need of them; but only on account of his goodness, and of the services they render to us " (I, q. 20, a. 2, ad 3). Of course, the profit that spiritual creatures draw from inferior beings is nothing in comparison with that love of God which draws them to him in order to live in company with the Three Persons. This point will be treated more fully in the question of the invisible missions.

§ III. God Is Provident

I. THE TEACHING OF FAITH

The entire Bible presupposes the basic assurance that all creatures are subject to the will of him who made them, and that this omnipotent will is exercised according to plans of infinite wisdom. God's activity is everywhere at work, but it is not arbitrary or disorderly. God foresees his action in the world. Without leaving anything to chance or committing any negligence, he takes care of his creatures and organizes their existence with all requisite prudence. His vigilance extends even to things of nature as well as to human beings, nations as well as individuals, personal events as well as the general history of the world. It is he who determines the laws which govern the natural order: the rotations of the stars (Jer 31,35-36), the frequency of the rains (Jer 5,24; Lev 26,4), the time of harvest (Lev 26,4; Deut 11,14; 28,12), the time of generations (Job 31,1), the limits imposed on the sea (Prov 8,29; Job 38,11). The entire universe obeys his orders and plans. " She (wisdom) deploys her strength from one end of the earth to the other, ordering all things for good " (Wis 8,1). But it is in relationship with men, who are of the highest value, that divine Providence manifests itself in a very special way. " For the Lord of all...himself made both small and great, and provides for all alike, " and the reason is simply because " he himself made both great and small " (Wis 6,7).

God is not satisfied with simply throwing humanity into existence; he is equally concerned with its progress. He leads it as a shepherd leads his flock to pasture. Thus it is that the political, military and religious events of Israel fall under the providential action of God, and in a general way, all the events of the history of nations are controlled by him. But even then it is not quite correct to say that God directs history. He personally intervenes in it; and above all in this sense that the entire history of Israel is conditioned by her fidelity or unfaithfulness to the gratuitous choice of which she had been the object. The sense in which God has personally entered in a special way into human history is of course his Incarnation. It is in Jesus that God's plan for humanity was revealed and carried out in a definitive manner. This is how the peculiarly Christian notion of providence must be explained. God wills the salvation of all men in Jesus Christ, and it is in terms of this salvation that he directs all the events of history. The eternal predisposition of this plan in God constitutes what is called Providence.

Thesis XI. *Universa, quae condidit Deus providentia sua tuetur atque gubernat, attingens a fine usque ad finem fortiter et disponens omnia suaviter. Omnia enim nuda sunt oculis ejus, ea etiam quae libera creaturarum actione futura sunt* (de fide, Vat. Conc. I, S. III, cap. I, Denz 1784).

Furthermore, by his providence God watches over and governs all the things that he made, reaching from end to end with might and disposing all things with gentleness. For " all things are naked and open to his eyes, " even those things that are going to occur by the free action of creatures *(of faith)*.

II.   THE UNDERSTANDING OF FAITH

1.   *The problem*

Many difficulties are raised by the affirmation of Providence. Because Providence is basically an action of God affecting man, it should be discernable within the framework of human existence. The majority of men, however, who deny the existence of God, arrive at this denial precisely because they do not see the execution of a wisely foreseen plan in the development of the world as well as in their own personal lives. Evil and suffering in all forms appear to them incompatible with a beneficent government. " In spite of all the arguments to which theologians and philosophers had recourse from the very beginnings, " writes G. Marcel, " atheism finds its permanent source of revitalization in the existence of evil and suffering among the innocent. " [6] The only reply that the Christian can make is that instead of running away from the problem he confronts it in its most puzzling expression: he keeps ever before his eyes and above his own sufferings the agony of Christ. Human history is marked forever by this most sorrowful of all " hours " that witnessed the death of Innocence itself. How could the providence of God allow Christ to fall into the hands of his avowed enemies? How can we understand the foreseeing action of God in this case which encompasses all the sufferings and injustices of all time?

2.   *The principle of the answer*

If we were tempted to forget it, it would be sharply brought back to our attention: God's providence is a mystery. We progress in faith, not in evidence. And yet, at the very moment when we penetrate into the

---

[6] G. Marcel, *L'athéisme contemporain* (Geneva: Labor et Fides, 1957) p. 90.

most obscure part of the mystery, it suddenly becomes enlightened
before our eyes with a supernatural light: Christ is a model of the Suffering
Servant! This is a scandal for the Jews, folly for the Greeks, the height
of weakness and stupidity, but for the Christian the supreme work of an
infinitely wise and powerful Love. It is out of love for men, out of
respect for his dignity and in order to allow him to be redeemed by one
like him, that God did not withdraw his Anointed One, Christ, from the
forces of evil. It is because Divine Providence was inspired by this
folly of love that it appeared to be wise in the eyes of the believer. This
is the principle that ought to govern all reflection: God acts out of love
and his omnipotent love is very prudent. We must therefore approach
all the problems raised by the affirmation of Divine Providence with this
truth.

3. *The act of Providence*

God is love. He is in love with his creature. This means that he wills
good for him. God himself gives the first of these goods by conferring
existence. To love a being and to create it is one and the same thing
for God. The love of God is creative by the fact that it causes the object
of its love to exist. It is at this height that we must place ourselves if
we want to explain the mystery of Providence. In fact, the idea of
Providence adds this element to that of creation: God not only loves his
creatures, but he loves them with a love of foresight that ultimately
expresses itself in definitive action.

What does this mean? Simply that God is not satisfied with willing
that creatures should simply exist, but foresees and creates their actual
perfection in existence, i.e. their orientation toward a goal. This progress
of creatures toward their goal is the object of divine providence. God is
prudent, i.e. he himself directs the progress of creatures toward their
end as a shepherd leads his flock to pasture. In his providential action,
however, God does not pursue some goal that is strange to him. God is
not prudent for his sake, since the goal of his action is immanent within
him; God is prudent for the sake of others by giving himself to them as
the supreme goal of their existence. It is for "love of his name" that
the Shepherd of men guides his faithful on just paths (Ps 23). In all
that he does, God acts by basing all his reasons for action upon himself.
"All that exists comes from him; all is by him and for him" (Rom 11,36).
God acts out of love of his love, without any egoism. He gives of himself
while drawing to himself, like glowing and attracting personalities among
whom one finds assurance, protection, and sincere consideration. This is
the manner in which God loves his creatures: He impels them toward

himself, attracts them to himself and in doing this, he loves them with
a prudent love. The nature of God's providence is to recognize and will
for his creatures this end or goal which he himself constitutes.

We must pause here for awhile. God in his goodness is the end of
the order foreseen by his providence. The reason for divine action
therefore is God himself. When we want to learn the " reasons " for
Providence, we must consider what we are asking: nothing less than
God's very essence. This is the presumption of which Job became
painfully aware, and putting his hand on his mouth he said: " I am the
man who obscured your designs with my empty-headed words, I have
been holding forth on matters I cannot understand, on marvels beyond
me and my knowledge " (Job 42,3). Actually, " who could ever know
the mind of the Lord, or who could ever be his counselor? " (Rom
11,33-34). The mystery of Providence is nothing else but the mystery of
God himself.

4. *The ways of Providence*

Lacking specific evidence on the ultimate end, we must consequently
show the paths followed by divine action in the *execution* of providential
designs. In willing himself as the last end of all things, God actually
wills each creature in its own existence. Since this last end, however, is
by nature transcendent, it leaves a vast opening for many secondary
ends, which are also means of attaining the ultimate end. There will
thus be as many ways of fitting into the order of providence as there are
ways of existing. The contingent and the necessary, the natural and
historical, rational and irrational, good and less good—everything that
exists reflects the transcendent providence of God according to its own
mode of existence. Thus everything is providential, *but not by the same
token*. In particular, among the things which happen providentially
some are willed by God, others only permitted, as we shall see later.

This incidentally allows us to state that providence works in a more
excellent way for the just than for the sinner, as St. Thomas shows.
Undoubtedly no one escapes the influence of Providence, though some
are affected in a more or less immediate and elevated fashion. That is
why the recognition of the providential will, such as it is revealed *for us*
through creatures and in given historical situations, requires in each case
a careful investigation that will consider not only the *fact* but also the
way which such an event can be ascribed to Providence.

5. *Recognition of providential action*

In this work of discernment, human reason is assisted by revelation.
Even though we do not clearly recognize the ultimate reason for

Providence, we nevertheless always know the *roads* or *ways* it follows.
" Make me to recognize your ways, " asks the Psalmist. What are the
ways foreseen by Providence that are supposed to be willed by human
beings?

There is first of all the way which follows the natural course of things.
God rules his creature according to the natural law which he has inscribed
within it from birth. When chemical bodies react according to their
properties, when plants grow according to their species, when the animal
follows the drive of his instinct, they all obey laws of Providence by
following the paths which God has drawn for them in advance. We are
familiar with the beautiful chapters of Ecclesiasticus (16,24—17,14) in
which the sacred writer shows us creatures subjected with precision to
laws dictated by God for the sake of the harmony of the entire group.

But the command of Providence is expressed quite naturally in a
more excellent way in the moral law. The voice of conscience indicates
the command willed by God in no uncertain terms. " Pagans who
never heard of the Law but are led by reason to do what the Law commands, may not actually ' possess ' the Law, but they can be said to
' be ' the Law. They can point to the substance of the Law engraved on
their hearts—they can call a witness, that is, their own conscience—they
have accusation and defense, that is, their own inner mental dialogue...
on the day when, according to the Good News I preach, God, through
Jesus Christ, judges the secrets of mankind " (Rom 2,14-16; cf. Sir
17,1-14).

Yet it is on this precise point that we encounter one of the most
confusing problems. Although Providence manifests itself in a prescription
of law, it is *accomplished* only in the effective observance of the law.
Providence actually concerns the acts in which men are concretely involved. But while irrational creatures necessarily follow the law inscribed
in their nature, man by his *freedom* has the power of straying from the
path foreseen by God. Thus it is easy to show how the just man obeys
Providence, but it is difficult to explain how the sinner relates to Providence. From one point of view, we must say that the sinner does not stray
from Providence, since God, who has created man with a free will which
is conditioned, of course, nevertheless respects this freedom. On the
other hand, he does stray from Providence by the fact that God does not
will the sin. God cannot will that a free man should not be free, nor can
he will sin. If the sin represents a lessening of being, this failure could
not be the deed of a creative will which manifests itself as creative only
by the rise and renewal of being; it must necessarily be the deed of a
fragile and fallible will, capable and culpable of this " vanity, " this

" nothingness " which will take away something of its perfection. The vanity of the sin not only causes the sinner to ignore Providence (insofar as he exists, he is willed by God), but hinders him from cooperating with it (God cannot be the cause of his sin). This then is the great difference between the saint and the sinner. It is in order to express this difference, which is demonstrable on the level of effects, and in order to mark the diversity of the modes according to which an act can be related to Providence, that theology distinguishes in God a " will-act " (from which springs all that is good) and a " permissive will " (source of evil). This point will later be taken up in more detail with regard to predestination.

6. *Providence and redemption*

Permission to sin does not express the basis of God's providence with regard to the sinner, and we must correct the excessively negative overtones of this point of view. For the sinner who is on the path of error, the love of God is powerful and ingenious enough to find ways which will lead him back, and these are the ways of mercy. Evil as such undoubtedly represents a complete loss. And it is a bit naive to say too glibly that God allows evil in order to draw from it greater good. In fact, the greatest good does not result from evil, but rather from God. Evil is only an occasion for God to *gratuitously* manifest the abundance of his mercy. The ways of God are not our ways: they belong only to him. Perhaps this is why he has prepared for the sinner who has strayed from the narrow and straight path of justice the great royal way of the Cross. Christ the Saviour is the mysterious route prepared from all eternity by Providence to lead all things into the unity of the kingdom of the redeemend. Thus, when God permits sin, when he allows Christ to be delivered up to death, his wisdom and his power do not undergo any stifling; for at the same time and by the very means of the sufferings of Christ, he prepares the salvation of the sinner. In Christ we have the revelation of a merciful Providence. The world is led by a merciful and just Providence; this is the undeniable fact that the scandal of the cross teaches us. Evil in itself does not remain less incomprehensible than the cross; but whatever incomprehensible elements it does contain are countered by the incomprehensible reaction of love that it evokes in God. " There where sins abounds, grace has superabounded. " Providence remains a mystery for us, but we understand that it is such not because of the apparent absurdity of the world and our life, but because its term, which is God, infinitely exceeds our understanding, and because in its principle it is inspired by this excessive love whose effect or extent could never be recognized by our heart left entirely to its own resources.

7. *Providence and evil*

It is in these perspectives that we must approach the problem of evil. The study of evil, incidentally, really has no place in a treatise on God. There is, however, such a close connection between the experience of evil and the affirmation of God, that they both shed light on each other: God affords evil its greatest depth at the same time that evil forces us to a more pure understanding of God and his work. Let us first of all briefly indicate what the evil of suffering (an abstraction drawn from the evil of deficiency) can teach us about God.

The first striking thing about primitive Hebrew thought is the radical contrast that it draws between evil and God. Evil appears only as *punishment*. Suffering necessarily strikes those who rise up against God, while it spares the just. Evil is the wages of sin; good, the fruit of justice. The sacred writers at first saw no other explanation. Yet in spite of its shortcomings, such a concept expresses a fundamental truth which can never be denied: Yahweh is a *just* God, and this means that he allows evil only as punishment or reparation in compensation for the injustices of men.

Yet we know that such an interpretation is in evident contrast with immediate experience: the wicked prosper, the just suffer. Then a new solution arose: evil is a *trial* intended to purify the just people. The idea of trial undoubtedly shows progress in that it forces one to adopt a more dynamic attitude with regard to evil. Passive submission to adversity is replaced by an active and voluntary tendency in which evil appears as a trial " to be overcome. " Evil experienced as a trial requires, in reaction, an internal transformation as well as an active battle against all its manifestations. It is in this active battle that the just man has an opportunity to penetrate deeper into the ways of Providence. Let us not forget God's Providence is not only an act of intellect, but also a creative act of the will and by this very fact it can be understood only in *active collaboration* with God coupled with an overcoming of self.

Actually the intervention of Providence does not exclude the exercise of created freedom. On the contrary, it is *implied and even demanded* and consequently on our level Providence cannot be grasped except within this active cooperation in which, at one and the same time, it is involved and revealed. Certainly, evil understood as a trial does not cease to underly the ultimate justice of God. In this regard Job represents the perfect example of a just man who in his misfortune remains faithful to the justice of God. This fidelity effects a purification in which moral values take a predominant place, but it also demands more than mere knowledge: it calls for *imitation* of the *holiness* of God, in the presence of which man declares himself a sinner. A trial thus becomes a revelation of the holiness of God.

But this solution again gives the reality of suffering a characteristic extrinsic to religious life as such. In the final analysis, suffering will be lived by the Hebrew nation as satisfaction for *sin,* personal or vicarious. In this perspective suffering will be taken up in the movement of charity and become by this very fact compatible with the innocence of the One who offered himself for the salvation of all. The Servant of Yahweh took upon himself the evils which are the consequence of his people's sins. Because of his innocence, he could offer God a true sacrifice and expiate the sins of the guilty; and because he is a man, all humanity was redeemed by him. This certainly manifests God's justice and holiness in a very striking way; but what is revealed about God with even greater clarity is the *merciful charity* of his providential action. Of course all this makes no sense unless it is bolstered by the hope of a happy immortality, which for the just man will constitute definitive compensation for the evils he has suffered in his life as well as reward for his fidelity to God who is Spirit.

All these answers which try to pinpoint the problem of evil more and more precisely evidently presuppose that man keeps himself in a state of openness toward the merciful love of God. But faith teaches us that man at the end of this present life can remain so hardened in his sins that they become unforgivable. It would therefore seem that the evil of sin, the most serious of all forms of evil, represents a definite defeat. How can we understand the Providence of God in regard to the reprobate, and conversely, how is it exercised in favor of the blessed? This is something that has to be examined more closely in the question of Predestination. [7]

§ IV. God Predestines

I. THE TEACHING OF FAITH

Predestination is a part of Divine Providence: it is Providence insofar as it directs men toward their supernatural end. In this mystery everything

[7] With regard to the problem of evil, cf. E. Borne, *Le Problème du mal* (Paris: PUF); J. Delanglade, *Le problème de Dieu* (Paris: Aubier, 1960) pp. 212-47; J. H. Nicolas, " La permission du péché, " *RT* 60 (1960) 5-38, 185-207, 509-47; C. Journet, *Le mal, essai théologique* (Desclée de Brouwer, 1960).

would be simple if all men would in fact attain beatitude. But the gospel very clearly points out the possibility of failure: God does not impose beatitude on anyone. He who made us without our help, cannot save us without our help. A man can reject grace and be damned through his own fault. This sin is not willed by God, but on the other hand if God wills the salvation of all men, how is it that certain men can obstruct his will? In what then does the mystery of predestination really consist?

1. *Holy Scripture: St. Paul*

The teaching of Scripture on this subject can be found essentially in two texts from St. Paul.

" We know that by turning everything to their good God cooperates with all those who love him, with all those that he has called according to his purpose. They are the ones he chose specially long ago and intended to become true images of his Son, so that his Son might be the eldest of many brothers. He called those he intended for this; those he called he justified and with those he justified he shared his glory " (Rom 8,28-30).

" Blessed be God the Father of our Lord Jesus Christ, who has blessed us with all the spiritual blessings of heaven in Christ. Before the world was made, he chose us, chose us in Christ to be holy and spotless, and to live through love in his presence, determining that we should become his adopted sons, through Jesus Christ for his own kind purposes " (Eph 1,3-5).

From an examination of these texts we see:

1) that the act of predestination *(proorizein)* is a voluntary determination which involves the destiny of humanity. This determination, foreseen and willed in advance, is an *act posited by God*. This act is more than simple knowledge; it is a choice, but this choice is not identical with its temporal execution. It is a decision decreed from all eternity *in God*. Finally, it is an act which is inspired entirely by the love of God, and it calls for a return of love.

2) It has pleased God to reveal this unfathomable plan to us in Christ Jesus, and we can recognize it by its effects. What is the object of this plan? The goal envisioned by predestination is the adoption of men in Christ Jesus, an adoption which must ultimately lead to final consummation in charity. To be predestined is to be willed by God in such wise as to become conformable to the image of his Son. St. Paul specifies that it is a question of free decision: God could have left men to their simple human destiny; he could have abandoned them to the dis-

grace into which their sins would have made them fall, but in reality he wills the salvation of all men in Christ. The first Epistle to Timothy forcefully expresses the thought of Paul on this subject: " To do this is right, and will please God our Saviour, he wants everyone to be saved and reach full knowledge of the truth. For there is only one God, and there is only one mediator between God and mankind, himself a man, Christ Jesus, who sacrificed himself as a ransom for them all. ... He is the evidence of this, sent at the appointed time " (1 Tim 2,3-6).

This universal salvific will of God determines the goal of predestination: the salvation of all men, obtained by conformity to the image of Christ. In what then does this conformity consist? Exegetes are divided on this point. For some it is final glory, for others, present grace. We think that it is glory: it is nothing else but a resemblance to Christ dead and resurrected, and this will be definitively acquired only in glory. Predestination actually governs an entire series of acts: vocation, justification, and glorification which lead to definitive salvation. Finally, the context of the Epistle to the Romans shows that St. Paul is not addressing pagans deprived of grace, but Christians who, being already saved in hope, " groan inwardly as they wait for...the redemption of (their) bodies " (Rom 8,24). [8]

The specific object of hope is eschatological salvation (Phil 3,21). Predestination, which lays the foundation for hope, also deals with the glory to come. It is important therefore to keep in mind that St. Paul speaks of predestination to salvation; he says nothing of predestination to perdition. Predestination is conceived in an exclusively positive and beneficent manner, and this idea arouses in Paul nothing but acts of thanksgiving.

3) To whom does predestination extend? To men chosen by God. St. Paul no longer views the choice here as a *division*, according to which some men will be saved and others will not. The choice is seen in its *content:* it bears upon " those who love. " St. Paul thus wants us to understand that we must formally discard the notion of destiny which would exclude free will: faith is the condition of salvation. The doctrine of St. John is no different in this regard: " God loved the world so much that he gave his only Son, so that everyone who believes in him may not be lost but may have eternal life " (Jn 3,16). Salvation, therefore, and the means of salvation are given to us in Christ; but this salvation must

---

[8] In this regard consult the classical commentaries on Paul's Epistle to the Romans by Prat, Lagrange, Huby. Cf. also the interesting discussion of K. Barth's theses by P. H. Bouillard in his book on *K. Barth*, Vol. 2, pp. 125-64.

be received, accepted, and this is where human freedom comes into play.

To speak of freedom is to speak of choice, and consequently of the possibility of refusal. *Suppose* that some men had revolted against God and hardened in their sin to the point of final impenitence. They are now lost, i.e. separated for ever from the love of God. Has their lot been foreseen and willed by God? St. Paul says nothing about this. The rejection of Israel which is treated in the Epistle to the Romans must not be confused with the predestination of individuals to glory or to definitive reprobation. This is evident from the method in which St. Paul explains how the rejection of the Jews—provisionary, of course—could be a part of the plan of salvation. The problem of reprobation will be explicitly raised later.

2. *The teaching of the Fathers: St. Augustine*

Prior to the crisis inaugurated by Pelagius, the Fathers hardly studied the mystery of predestination or reprobation " from God's point of view, " as did St. Augustine. Without denying the primacy of divine love in the work of salvation, they dwelt instead on the mystery of grace within us. On the other hand, when they finally took to battling against the blind destiny of the Stoics and against Marcionism, that hidden Manicheism of the gnostics, they were interested only in giving weight and value to the statement that everything is grace, that man is not subject to a blind fate, but that he acts freely and will be rewarded according to his merits. They still did not try to investigate the order of divine intentions. [9]

Among the Latin Fathers the problem arises again with St. Augustine, whose testimony has exercised the greatest influence on western thought. St. Augustine clearly approaches the question on God's level. By predestination he understands " the foreknowledge and the preparation of God's kindnesses, whereby they are most certainly delivered, whoever they are that are delivered " (*De Praed.*, II,35).

Predestination therefore is more than foreknowledge; it is a pre disposition. Arguing against Pelagius, St. Augustine underlined the absolute gratuity of predestination. The reason for predestination is not the prevision of merits, but simply the mercy of God. Merits are the effect, not the motive of predestination. Under such conditions, the reprobate cannot be predested: neither to good, because God would have led them there infallibly; nor to evil, for God could never positively

[9] For the teaching of the Greek Fathers cf. H. D. Simonin, " *Prédestination,* " *DTC* 12, 2815-32.

force a person to sin. God allows sin; he does not will it. And it is because of this prevision of either original sin or the loss of justification that God refuses the grace of predestination. Once having admitted that all men belong to the " *massa damnata* " from birth, it can be understood that God without any injustice can leave certain souls in their state of corruption by not granting them the grace of justification.

But the weakness of St. Augustine's doctrine (according to the opinion of good exegetes) is that it does not give a satisfactory explanation of the part that God actually and freely plays in the salvation of all men. Yet if his will is to have any meaning at all, it should mean that all men (at least the adults) have been placed by God in an efficacious way on the road to salvation. " This principle does not mean that all have been justified, but that all have received the *initium salutis.* " [10] Here on the theological level lies a weakness which is going to influence the evolution of this doctrine.

3. *The doctrine of the Church*

The death of St. Augustine did not put an end to the arguments on grace. Opponents and partisans maintained and hardened their positions: the predestinationists rose up against the semi-pelagians. Among the former was a certain Lucidus, a priest from Gaul. He had to subscribe to the decisions of the Council of Arles, held in 475, and among other things he had to reject the many erroneous opinions that he held: that Christ did not die for all; that divine foreknowledge forced some men to die the death of the soul, and therefore that some were destined to death and others predestined to life. In 529, the Second Council of Orange, presided over by St. Caesarius and subsequently approved by Pope Boniface II, confirmed the following: 1) the absolutely gratuitous character of predestination to good; 2) the impossibility of predestination to evil (without however taking any stand on the nature of this evil); 3) the possibility of salvation for all baptized individuals who would wish to work it out (Denz 200). We know that this council, dominated entirely by the influence of St. Augustine, has considerable importance: it consolidated the faith.

The controversies on predestination arose again in Gaul during the 9th century, following upon the theses advanced by a vagabond monk of Saxon origin named Gotescalc. He seems to have professed a twofold

---

[10] G. Bavaud, " La doctrine de la prédestination et de la réprobation d'après saint Augustin et Calvin, " *REA* 5 (1959) 438.

predestination: that of the elect to glory by pure grace, and that of the reprobate to eternal death by a just judgment. In addition he conferred upon this double predestination a character of necessity which rendered it still more rigid. By the same token the universality of the salvific will of God was strongly restricted. As for Christ, he did not die on the cross for the reprobate. Gotescalc was condemned many times, and after long discussion his theses were rejected by the Council of Quierzy in 853. The council rejected his theory of twofold predestination and maintained the unique predestination of the elect to eternal life. As for the reprobate, God foresees their loss, but he does not predestine them to perish; he only decides in advance the punishment which will be inflicted upon them (Denz 316). The council duly recalled that man is endowed with free will (Denz 317); that God wills the salvation of all men, and that the loss of the reprobate is their own fault; finally that Christ suffered for all, even though all are not saved (Denz 319).

The Council of Quierzy, which defined the sentiments of the Church in Soissons, had only regional importance. Its conclusions were not admitted by all. They were distorted into a very severe interpretation by the metropolitans of Lyon, Valence, and Arles, together with their suffragans united in Council at Valence in 855. This gathering gave the Fathers an occasion to condemn the theses of John Scotus Eriugena, who denied predestination *ad poenam*. The Council taught that God foresaw both evil and good, rewards and punishments, but his foreknowledge did not impose upon things a necessity of nature (Denz 321). In this foreknowledge, God predestines the elect to life and the wicked to death; but by "death" we must understand the evil of punishment, not the evil of sin, for God can predestine only to those things that he has created. Therefore, while predestination to life precedes merits, predestination to punishment is preceded by demerit (Denz 322). In spite of these specifications, predestination *ad mortem* was considered too severe. It was rejected by the assembly of French Bishops gathered in Council at Tuzey in 860, a council which provisorily put an end to the arguments on predestination. Four principal points were retained and proposed for the faith of the faithful: " God desires the salvation of all men; free will still remains after the Fall, but it had to be saved and healed by the grace of God; divine predestination selects some individuals *ex massa perditionis* and predestines them to life out of pure mercy, the rest of the *massa* is left to itself *(relicta)*; finally, Christ died for all men. " [11]

[11] C. J. Hefele-Leclercq, *Histoire des conciles*, 4, 1, 229.

In 1053, the symbol of Leo IX will simply mention that God predestined only the good, although he foresaw the good as well as the bad (Denz 348).

The errors of Protestantism forced the Council of Trent to make in regard to decrees concerning justification some precisions that are of capital importance for our subject. Luther denied the free will as well as the necessity of good works for salvation. Calvin on the other hand professed a positive will of perdition in God: " Nor should it be thought absurd to affirm that God not only foresaw the fall of the first man, and the ruin of his posterity in him, but also arranged all by the determination of his own will. " " I inquire again, how it came to pass that the fall of Adam, independent of any remedy, should involve so many nations with their infant children in eternal death, but because such was the will of God. " [12] The distinction between permissive will and will-act is thus erased. In opposition to these heresies, the Council affirmed: 1) that free will remains after sin, and its positive cooperation is necessary for grace to accomplish its work (Denz 814-815); 2) that God does not cause evil properly and directly; he permits it (Denz 816); 3) that he does not predestine to evil and does not necessarily refuse his grace to those who are not predestined to eternal life (Denz 827); 4) that no one knows whether or not he is predestined (rejection of fatalism) (Denz 805). These canons have a definite importance; but it is obvious that they touch on the problem of predestination only incidentally.

Finally, let us cite the condemnation pronounced in 1653 against the 5th proposition drawn from the *Augustinus* of Jansenius, according to which: " It is semi-Pelagian to say that Christ dies or sheds his blood for all men without exception. " The popes declared this proposition heretical: all men have the objective means for salvation (Denz 1096).

Thesis XII. *Deus in misericordia sua, praedestinavit salvandos in Salvatore ad gratiam in gloriam; reprobavit alios, sed neminem praedestinavit ad culpam* (de fide).

In his mercy, God has predestined to grace and glory in the Saviour those who must be saved. He has rejected the others, but he has not predestined anyone to sin *(of faith)*.

---

[12] J. Calvin, *Institutes of the Christian Religion*, Bk. 3, chap. 23, vii.

II. THE UNDERSTANDING OF FAITH

1. *The problem*

From God's point of view, the certitude is incontestable. St. Paul's statement must be taken in its strict meaning: God predestined some men to the happy life. God has foreseen and willed that some men chosen by him are ordered to glory and are effectively provided with the means of obtaining it; this is the effect of his creative love. Nothing can obstruct the realization of this love, for God is omnipotent and his knowledge just like his will in no way depends on the free will of man, especially since the end foreseen belongs to the supernatural order.

But if the *fact* is incontestable, the *reason* is unknown. It is impossible for us to imagine the nature of divine freedom. The majority of our difficulties stem precisely from this, that we imagine divine freedom along the lines of human freedom. This is why it is impossible to explain how both can concur in positing one and the same action: there is one " freedom " too many. If God orientates me infallibly toward the goal which he has specified, like an arrow shot at a target, I am no longer free to choose my goal. My destiny is no longer in my own hands. Moreover, if the sovereign decision of this Other has been predetermined, my temporal existence has no meaning. Even before beginning in time, my future was entirely determined; I am no more than a piece of luggage provided with a sticker, waiting to be sent to a destination which I have neither foreseen nor willed.

In order to understand this, however, we must seek a different explanation. Let us begin with the facts, i.e. begin with what we are trying to prove (human freedom in practice) and not with an incomprehensible mystery (divine freedom in its superhuman practice). Now we can ask whether the analysis of this freedom does not force us to state that its exercise betrays a lack of autonomy, is not explained entirely by itself, and therefore requires a cause. We will then say everything that happens in the world, including my most free act, has God for its cause and is consequently willed by him. The intellect will therefore be redirected from the effect toward the cause but without pretending to understand this cause.

2. *Human freedom and its limits*

At the very outset let us accept human freedom as a fact. Let us specify that this freedom does not consist only in dominating and choosing different means at man's disposal for the attainment of his end. Man does not orientate himself towards a necessarily predetermined goal, like a plant which develops according to its species. Because he is capable of self-awareness in regard to values, a person can will himself and can develop himself as he pleases. He is therefore free in his destiny in the degree to which he does and becomes what he wills: to be a saint or a failure. But the free act by which the spirit engages in and defines its destiny is not an absolutely pure nor perfect act. For if the spirit could will *what* it wanted to be and thereby become that object, it still could not will its *own being* to the point of freely being its own action. Existence is given to it; it is not free to be or not to be. Its act of existence is not its free act. This act depends on God. Human freedom does exist, but it is not absolute; it subsists because of a transcendent cause.

This conclusion is inevitable: the most free act of will, in the precise measure in which it exists, exists by God. At each moment, God *causes* this will *to exist*, this same will which freely determines itself for good or evil. Understood in this fashion, creation does not in any way suppress freedom of human action. Essentially freedom of the spirit holds the power of constant control over its action. I exercise this profession and not another, I have certain political preferences; my liberty consists in this, that I at any moment do whatever I please.

This freedom furthermore is inalienable by the very fact that a relationship of contingency exists between my will and the actions I perform. I am therefore free to do what I will, *presupposing that I exist*, and this is where the divine will enters. It is God's accomplishment and not my own that I *exist* and can perform various other kinds of actions. I have the potency to be any kind of individual, but this potency depends upon the creative freedom which has caused me to exist. In giving existence to my freedom so that all my actions are contingently related to my will, not only is God incapable of destroying my liberty, but he actually gives it existence.

The operation by which God sustains human action ought to be considered as a prolongation of his creative activity. To consider its origin, this action stems entirely from a created will and entirely from the divine will. And still the efficacy of the created will never equals that of the primary will. The action of the created will is *particular:* it consists in self-determination. The action of God is *total*, it consists in giving existence to a will that is self-determining. God is never the cause of voluntary determination without being at the same time the cause of the will from which this determination proceeds. We can therefore never attribute the responsibility of an act to him without specifying: insofar as he caused this act to spring from a will created by him as freely and immediately responsible for its actions. [13] Nothing in human experience can help us imagine such efficacy.

3. *The act of predestination*

These reflections lead us to the mystery of predestination. It suffices for us now to elevate what has been said about the exercise of freedom in general to the supernatural order. Predestination bears upon eternal happiness and that is a goal which surpasses the natural forces of human reason as well as the human will. But we can learn more about it through the analogous use of information gathered from the natural order of things. The fact that God predestines indicates that a certain order of execution corresponds to the divine intentions. According to this order 1) God gives existence to a specific man endowed with freedom; 2) God wills that this man should freely turn to Christ; 3) God wills him glory a a reward for his merits. The difference between this and what we have observed in the natural order consists in the fact that man could not decide by himself in favor of salvation without the help of grace, i.e. without the supplement of energy that God grants him in consideration of the merits of Christ. The call to grace, justification, and glorification are all executed in terms of a predestination decreed in God from all eternity.

This act of predestination evidently eludes the grasp of our intellect, which is satisfied with simply affirming its existence. But in order to avoid any misunderstanding, we must reject the illusions of imagination which would deny the existence of predestination. Let us first of all recall that predestination is an act which takes place outside of time. The created spirit perdures, it exists in time. God, however, does not exist in time. Still let us not imagine him as a sort of emperor of the world, a little more powerful than man, a little more clever, who has willed yesterday or the day before that which I am doing today. Eternity is not measured by human standards of duration, and although " before " and " after " are determinations of duration, we must say that God has

---

[13] J. H. Nicolas is correct in his observation that motor action, which moves to activity, should not be confused with creative action, which produces existence. They differ by their effects. But since action presupposes existence, it is related to existence as to its principle. God creates an existent by granting it existence; this existent not only possesses a nature, but also freedom of action by reason of its free will. Motion thus presupposes creation. This does not mean that God chooses *in my stead;* he does not assume responsibility for my action, but everything I will and even myself in the act of willing—all this he wills in an act that underlies all human activity because it reaches to the very root of existence. (Cf. J. H. Nicolas, " La permission du péché, " *RT* 60 (1960) 12).

not willed final salvation before our existence. When Scripture teaches that God has willed in advance whatever he effectively produces, this means: 1) God does not exist in time; he lives in eternity with no " before " or " after "; 2) whatever we do at each moment exists only by his will, and that God does not have to wait for me to decide in order to know what I will do. Nevertheless eternity does not suppress the experience of time for me.

There is still another illusion that must be removed: the word " destination " presupposes a distinction between the end and the means. We notice in reality an order of *consequence* between final happiness and the means granted to achieve it. This is why happiness appears to be a reward for merits that the Christian has acquired in time. But this order of consequence, in which merit seems to take on the *raison d'être* of final reward, is realized only on the level of effects. It does not exist in God. We must not say that God wills the end before the means, as if the divine will dealing with reward was the cause of the divine will dealing with justification; if that were the case, then the graces granted to the reprobate would make no sense. Nor must we say that God grants happiness because of the merits of man, for then there would be a passivity in God, a dependence upon human choice. But what we must say is that God wills that the merits of man should be the cause of his final reward. The will-act by which God predestines a man does not aim at any end or goal external to God: it is an act which has no other motive than infinite love, i.e. God himself. " The merits of a saint are not the cause of the divine act, nor even its reason for existence, they are the cause of happiness obtained by predestination. " [14]

We know that Molina [15] in his anxiety to preserve human freedom thought that God decided human destiny only *after* having foreseen, in his " middle knowledge, " what a man would do if he were placed in particular circumstances and helped by certain graces. The merit foreseen by this middle knowledge thus becomes the motive of pre-destination. The Church does not forbid this pattern of thought, provided that one maintain an absolutely gratuitous first grace as necessary for justification. But such an explanation complicates matters without really casting any true light; it presupposes that human consent to grace as such is independent of the divine will. By this very fact it makes divine provision dependent upon the choice that man will make once he

[14] H. Paissac, *Initiation théologique* 2, p. 133.

[15] Cf. E. Vansteenberghe, " Molinisme, " *DTC* 10, 2094-2187 and the classical work by R. de Scoraille, *F. Suarez* (Paris, 1912).

is placed in specific circumstances. It does not explain God's prevision of this consent which can be induced neither by the divine will (hypothetically) nor by the human will (of itself, undetermined), nor by circumstances, (nonconstraining). Instead it grants to circumstances a role which risks ruining human freedom as well as leaving the favorable or unfortunate circumstances—foreseen by God for this or that individual— entirely without an explanation.

4. *The rejection of those eventually damned*

Although everything about predestination seems clear, reprobation still stands in the shadow cast upon it by the mystery of evil. We must admit that everything will not be explained because evil of itself is inexplicable. Reprobation deals with a sinner who is hardened in evil to the point of final impenitence. Just like everything else that exists, sinful man depends upon the creative will. But strictly speaking, we cannot interpret this will as predestination. God can predestine only to the things he has made. He cannot therefore predestine man to sin. At most he can will the punishment which will be the just deserts of sin, and it is in this sense we can say that he rejects or condemns.

Supposing that some man would be reprobate, this would mean: 1) that God places this man into existence with his freedom; 2) God does not will the sin committed by this man, for since this sin of itself is a lack of existence, it would not require the intervention of a transcendent cause; therefore we say that God *allows* the sin; 3) God wills that punishment should be the consequence of sin. The difficulty here arises from the fact that man can turn toward the supernatural end only with the help of grace, and that he cannot miss this end except by being deprived of an efficacious grace. But in point of fact he has not been deprived of every grace. He has been called to salvation like every other man; he has received graces sufficient to achieve this salvation, i.e. the real power to do good. [16] He has failed to give his consent when it was required. This man himself is to blame for his sin, and therefore he alone is reponsible for the chastisement that follows, which consists essentially in the conscious rejection of God's love.

The impenitent sinner who rejects the love of God, exists by God, and the necessary consequence of his act exists also, i.e. it is known and willed by God. This is the meaning of the word " reprobation. " Here

---

[16] The distinction between sufficient grace and efficacious grace will be taken up in another volume of the series: *Grace of Christ*. Here let us indicate that by sufficient grace we mean a real, subjective, and in this sense " efficacious " grace; in relationship to other graces, this one is simply sufficient.

again the *sequence* between the sin and its punishment exists on the level of effects and not in God. God does not will punishment because of sin (this would posit passivity in God); nor does he permit it because of the punishment which he has specified (this would render the evil necessary). By reason of his justice, he wills that punishment should be the consequence of sin. God wills that all men should be saved, i.e. that they freely accept salvation, and he cannot will the contrary; those who damn themselves prove this truth *a contrario*.

5. *Predestination and reprobation*

We see that there is no parallel between predestination and reprobation. Divine causality is not exercised in the same way in each case. " Reprobation differs in its causality from predestination. This latter is the cause both of what is expected in the future life by the predestined —namely, glory—and of what is received in this life—namely, grace. Reprobation, however, is not the cause of what is in the present—namely, sin; but it is the cause of abandonment by God. It is the cause, however, of what is assigned to the future—namely, eternal punishment. But guilt proceeds from the free will of the person who is reprobate and deserted by grace. In this way the world of the prophet is true—namely, " Destruction is thy own, O Israel " (*STh* I, q. 23, a. 3, ad 2).

This disproportion between predestination and reprobation removes every arbitrary character from the choice of the elect. God pays no attention to person, and on the other hand, he never commands the impossible.

The choice of the predestined is not a division; God calls all men to salvation, but mankind itself separates into two camps for or against Christ.

The choice of the predestined is not a preselection of a great or small number of favored out of the " *massa perditionis.* " God could have proceeded thus without any injustice, but he willed to save all men in Christ, i.e., to grant to all the real power to orient themselves toward the salutary good and therefore toward the " *massa redempta.* " It is exceptional that some should be lost, and if this is so, they themselves bear the responsibility for their sin.

Are the predestined not preferred? Does not God love them more than others? Certainly, but we must understand this principle of predilection correctly. God's love knows no change or degree: it is infinite. God loves some more than others, the predestined more than the reprobate, in the sense that he grants more good to them. They are loved more, they are *better* than the other because they actually *are* such, having

freely received more good.   We are thus led to face the facts.   Theological
reason affirms this fact, but when it tries to explain divine choice by
reasons or motives, it falters.   " Why he draws one and draws not another,
do not desire to judge, if thou desirest not to err, " remarks St. Augustine
(*In Jn*, Tr XXVI, 2).   God's preferences are not exclusive.   God does
not choose one man in preference *to another*, as a ruler might choose his
ministers in preference to others.   The divine choice *gives existence* to the
elect individual who converts, just as (without however being the cause
of his sin) it *gives existence to and tolerates* the sinner who damns himself.
Yet God prefers both elect and sinners to things that do not exist.   Every
existent is an island of freedom, and the existence of each one presupposes
an infinite love.   The happiness of the blessed can be explained only by
this love, and the suffering of the reprobate, who harden in their rejection
of love though they naturally tend toward good, likewise has no other
explanation except in relationship to this infinite love. [17]

The mystery remains.   Sin is a mystery, yet God " allows " it.
Let's not say too glibly that he permits it in view of a greater good, or in
order to make his justice more manifest.   It is not too clear exactly to
what ulterior good the existence of the damned can contribute.   Furthermore God manifests his justice in a much more striking way in the just
than in the damned.   While remaining on the order of reality, let us
simply state only so much as is accessible to us, viz., that sin springs
from a fallible or weak will; that a better world could have existed, but
taking everything into consideration, the world such as it is could not be
better than it *is*; and that even in its imperfection the world still proves
the existence of a prime Lover.   Everything else remains a mystery.
Have I been predestined?   I have no certitude other than that of hope.
I am not certain of obtaining salvation, but I am certain of tending
towards it, so much so that I can hope for it, if I at least accomplish
what God expects of me and if he will give me the power to do it.

[17] On this theme consult the admirable conference by Lacordaire (Conference
72 at Notre Dame de Paris).

CONCLUSION

All the truths surrounding the mystery of God are given simultaneously in the faith. But theological reason which tries to grasp them and explain them can do so only piecemeal. It consequently must begin by putting them in order. The first care of human reason was to demonstrate or show that God exists. From the theological point of view, this truth actually constitutes the basis of all the others. " For, " remarks St. Thomas, " if we do not demonstrate that God exists, all consideration of divine things is necessarily suppressed " (*Contra Gentes* I,9). Every effort of human reason that the theologian puts at the service of faith depends on the rational knowledge that God exists. This does not mean that philosophical demonstration of the existence of God should be at the source of all religious and supernatural knowledge of God. Quite the contrary, the theologian undertakes this demonstration only with the intention of explaining faith; he himself believes that God exists, not because of the proofs that can be adduced, but because God himself has revealed his existence. In the degree to which it is a participation in the knowledge which God has of himself, faith takes precedence over the explanation of faith. On the *level of explanation*, however, the demonstration of the existence of God is necessarily presupposed at the beginning of every theological process. If human reason cannot effectively open itself to the recognition of the Absolute, it could say nothing coherent or intelligible about him.

Theology therefore has taken its first step in proving that God exists. It establishes this proof by beginning with the existence of the most humble things of this world and by showing that these things do not subsist at all without a primary cause which is God. The purification which is then imposed in order to manifest the transcendence of the divine existence only reinforces the central affirmation: God exists in the sense that he alone is the pure act of being, simple, infinite, unique, immutable and eternal, absolutely perfect. God is *he who is*.

A second step leads reason to state that God has knowledge and volition. Upon reflection, no longer upon the existence of things in general but upon human existence in particular, we have been able to show that a necessary link joins thought and volition on the one hand, and being on the other. Thus did we discover the possibility of reducing spiritual activity to the act of being. Reason found itself thereby in a position to explain the action by which God reveals himself in his omnipotence, in his inscrutable providence, in his justice and his mercy, and in his infinite love for humanity. In God is verified the pure act of knowing and willing: God is *he who acts*.

Obviously nothing in these affirmations surpasses the conclusions of a natural theology. A metaphysic fully conscious of its presuppositions would be equally correct in concluding to the existence of a God perfect in intellect and will. The perspectives of theology, however, are radically different.

First of all, they are different to the degree in which the conclusions are introduced as an answer to a revelation concerning the supernatural destiny of man and his eternal salvation. Philosophers would be hard put to sustain the existence of a provident and loving God. But in the eyes of a theologian this providence and love necessarily take on a new meaning and manifest themselves with a clarity unknown even to the most profound religious thought from the moment of their first appearance at the beginning of the salvation of humanity in Jesus Christ. Although the conclusions remain substantially the same, the realities and the events which they explain are radically different.

But above all, the singularity of the theological perspective derives from the fact that its conclusions are contained in a revelation about the mystery of God in himself. A new level opens up for theology: that of the consideration of the Mystery of the Trinity. The coming of Christ has changed the destiny of man by unveiling to him the depths of God. Where knowledge of human nature as such can teach us no more about God, knowledge of Jesus Christ makes us enter into communion with the Father, Son and Spirit. The God of Jesus Christ therefore is the object which is now offered to the theologian.

Nevertheless, we would err in believing that in passing from the consideration of One to that of the Trinity, theological reason passes from a purely natural knowledge of God to supernatural knowledge, and that this latter renders the former superfluous. In reality, it is the same mystery which remains under investigation throughout the entire tract on God, at least from the theologian's point of view. The God of Jesus Christ is none other than the God of Abraham, the God of Creation. There is only one God. Whatever the theologian has said of the One God will constantly underlie his statement about the Trinity. When we profess the existence of *one God alone* in Three Persons, we include the affirmation that the Three Persons constitute one God. This means that the understanding of the Trinitarian Mystery can be achieved only in view of the certitudes acquired about the nature of God. In order to speak of them, human reason will necessarily use the same language with which it spoke of him who is. The understanding of the God of Jesus Christ will give way to that of the one God. Conversely, what revelation teaches or will teach us about God will deepen whatever we learn from now on by means of human reason illumined by faith. The affirmation of the One God actually does not have the same meaning for the philosopher as it does for the theologian. For the latter it is infinitely richer. But the deepening is possible only if the theologian, in raising himself to the affirmation of him who is, tells us more than just the existence of a Cause of the world. He ought to tell us God's proper name. To hear this name, in the same spirit in which Moses heard it is to have the glory of God pass over one's face.

Genesis

1	*3*	31
18		15
18	*27*	54
25		15

Exodus

3	*5*	53
3	*6*	54
3	*14-15*	30
19	*12-13*	54
20	*2*	65
33		15

Leviticus

19	*2*	54
19	*2, 7, 20*	54
20	*3, 7*	53
21	*8*	54
21	*22*	54
22	*2, 32*	53
22	*9, 31*	54
22	*31-38*	54
26	*4*	118

Deuteronomy

4	*5-6*	96
4	*12*	32
6	*4*	66
11	*14*	118
28	*12*	118
32	*39*	31

Judges

| 24 | *2-3* | 64 |

1 Samuel

| 26 | *19* | 66 |

2 Samuel

| 6 | *7* | 54 |

1 Kings

| 22 | *19* | 15 |

Judith

| 5 | *6-9* | 64 |

Job

28	*24*	95
28	*38-39*	96
31	*1*	118
34	*14-15*	52
38	*11*	118
42	*2-3*	54
42	*3*	121

Psalms

1		96
11	*4*	95
19	*8*	96
23		120
33	*15*	95
53	*2*	16
79	*9*	116
90	*2-4*	74
94	*1-2*	95
94	*9-11*	96
102	*27*	74
104	*29-30*	52
106	*8*	116
119		96
136	*1-9*	108
139		95
139	*4*	96
145	*9*	108

Proverbs

8	*22-31*	96
8	*29*	118
15	*11*	95
16	*2*	95

Wisdom

6	*7*	118
7	*22-31*	96
8	*1*	118
10		96
11	*24*	108
13		16
13	*1*	32
13	*4*	22
13	*5*	22
17		52

Sirach (Ecclesiasticus)

16	*24—17 14*	122
17	*1-14*	122
24	*3*	96
24	*3-6*	96
24	*8*	96
44		96

Isaiah

1	*4*	53
5	*29*	53
6		15, 53, 54
6	*4*	54
6	*5*	53
7	*18-19*	66
10	*6*	66
10	*17*	54
10	*20*	53
16	*20*	53
31	*3*	52
40	*8-26*	96
40	*19-20*	67
40	*20*	54
40	*25*	53
41	*4*	74
41	*14*	53, 54
41	*21*	67, 116
42	*21-29*	95
43	*9-10*	74
44	*1*	74
44	*6*	32
44	*9, 20*	67
44	*24-28*	96
45	*14*	32
45	*14-21*	32
45	*15*	66
45	*18*	65
45	*21-22*	67, 74
46	*3-4*	75
46	*9*	32
48	*12*	32
48	*13*	96
49	*15*	109

Jeremiah

2	27	67
3	9	67
5	15-17	66
5	24	118
10	1-6	67
14	21	116
16	20	67
31	3	109
31	35-36	118

Hosea

| 1 | 9 | 31 |

Amos

1—2		66
4	13	66
5	8	66
6	11	66

Matthew

3	17	110
5	24	111
5	43-48	112
6	18	79
7	21	105
11	27	96
17	15	110

Mark

12	26	112
12	29-32	67
12	33	111

Luke

5	9	54
6	26-35	112
11	42	111

John

1	3	96
1	12	110
3	16	110, 127
4	24	52

8	58	33, 74
13	14	111
13	34	111
15	4-9	111
15	16	112
15	19	110
15	22-27	111
17	21	111
17	23	111

Acts of the Apostles

14	15	24
17	23	24
17	27	24
17	30-31	24

Romans

1		16
1	18-20	26
1	19-21	23
2	14-16	122
5	5	112
5	7-8	112
8	24	127
8	28-30	126
8	29	110
8	39	110
11	33-34	121
11	36	120

1 Corinthians

1	21	23
1	30	96
8	3	111

2 Corinthians

| 1 | 3 | 112 |
| 5 | 7 | 16 |

Galatians

| 4 | 6 | 112 |
| 4 | 8 | 23 |

Ephesians

| 1 | 3-5 | 126 |
| 1 | 3-4 | 55 |

1	9-10	108
1	16	96
2	4	110
2	9	112
4	6	20
5	1-2	111, 112
5	25	112

Philippians

| 3 | 21 | 127 |

Colossians

1	13	110
1	15-20	96
3	12	110
3	12-14	112

1 Thessalonians

1	4	110
1	9	24
4	5	23

2 Thessalonians

| 1 | 8 | 23 |
| 2 | 13 | 110 |

1 Timothy

| 2 | 3-6 | 127 |
| 6 | 16 | 16 |

Hebrews

| 4 | 13 | 95 |

1 John

1	3	108
3	1	110
3	24	112
4	7	110
4	12	16
4	13	112
4	16	110
4	19	111

Revelation (Apocalypse

| 1 | 17 | 74 |

Quotations from the *Jerusalem Bible* (© 1966 by Darton, Longman & Todd, London, and Doubleday and Company, Inc., Garden City, New York) used by permission of the publishers.

INDEX OF COUNCILS AND DOCUMENTS

Councils

Arles (in 475), 129
Lateran IV (in 1215), 56, 80
Nicaea, 68
Orange II (in 529), 129
Quierzy (in 853), 130
Toledo XV (in 688), 56

Trent, 131
Tuzey (in 860), 130
Valence (in 855), 130
Vatican I, 56
Vatican II, 68
Vienne (in 1311), 17

Documents

Encycl. *Æterni Patris*, 26
 Humani generis, 93
 Pascendi, 26
 Studiorum ducem, 26

Motu Proprio *Doctoris Angelici*, 80
Oath against *Modernism*, 26
Syllabus of Erros, 56
Symbol of Leo IX in 1053, 131

INDEX OF PROPER NAMES

A

Albright (W. F.), 31
Amalric (Amaury) de Bene, 56
Ambrose (Saint), 34
Anselm (Saint), 19, 20
Aristotle, 29, 34, 39
Athanasius (Saint), 24, 33
Athenagoras, 24, 68
Augustine (Saint), 34, 55, 75, 80, 103, 128, 129, 138

B

Barth (K.), 111, 127
Basil (Saint), 24
Bavaud (G.), 129
Bergson (H.), 29
Bernard (Saint), 34
Boethius, 75
Boismard (E.), 32
Boniface II (Pope), 129
Borne (E.), 125
Bouillard (H.), 7, 24, 127
Branchereau, 17
Buber (M.), 54

C

Caesarius (Saint), 129
Calvin, 129
Claudel (P.), 98
Clement of Alexandria (Saint), 33
Cyril of Alexandria (Saint), 34

D

Delanglade (J.), 125
Denis (Pseudo-), 80
Descartes (R.), 20, 101
Dhorme (E.), 31

Duméry (H.), 71
Dupont (J.), 23

E

Eckart (Master), 56
Ephrem (Saint), 33, 34, 68
Epiphanius (Saint), 68
Eriugena (John Scotus), 130
Eunomius, 16, 24
Eusebius, 33, 75

G

Garrigou-Lagrange (R.), 63
Gilson (E.), 2, 19, 26, 34, 38, 41, 42, 78, 115
Gotescalc, 129
Gregory the Great (Saint), 75
Gregory of Nazianzen (Saint), 24, 33, 34
Gregory of Nyssa (Saint), 24, 33, 34

H

Hefele-Leclercq (C. J.), 130
Heidegger (M.), 10, 29
Hilary (Saint), 34, 75
Hippolytus Romanus (Saint), 68
Huby (J.), 127

I

Ignatius (Saint), 68
Imschoot (P. van), 80
Irenaeus (Saint), 17, 24, 33, 68

J

Jacob (E.), 53, 109
Jansenius, 131
Jerome (Saint), 34

John Chrysostom (Saint), 24
John of Damascus (Saint), 17, 34
Journet (C.), 125

K

Kant (E.), 27
Kunsin (R.), 33

L

Lacordaire (H. D.), 138
Lactantius, 68
Lagrange (M. J.), 127
Lucidus, 129
Luther (M.), 131

M

Malebranche (N.), 17
Malevez (L.), 6
Marcel (G.), 8, 119
Maritain (J.), 21, 26, 41
Marx (K.), 28
Michaeli (F.), 16, 79
Milone, 49
Minucius Felix, 24
Molina, 135
Moré-Pontgibaud (Ch. de), 88
Motte (A. R.), 2
Mouroux (J.), 76

N

Neher (A.), 16
Nicolas (J. H.), 125, 134

O

Origen, 33, 34, 35, 68

P

Paissac (H.), 41, 47, 135
Pascal (B.), 76
Pelagius, 128
Pius XI (Pope), 26
Pius XII (Pope), 26
Plato, 34, 72
Prat (F.), 127
Prestige (G. L.), 55

R

Rahner (K.), 7, 67, 109
Rosmini (A.), 17

S

Schweitzer (E.), 33
Scoraille (R. de), 135
Simonin (H. D.), 128
Spicq (C.), 112
Steenberghen (F. van), 39

T

Tatian, 55
Tertullian, 24, 34, 55, 68
Theodore of Mopsuestia, 34
Theophilus (Saint), 24
Thomas (Saint), 1, 3, 11, 25, 38, 41,
    47, 48, 71, 83, 84, 85, 86, 87, 88,
    101, 117, 121, 137, 139

V

Vacant (J. M. A.), 76
Valensin (A.), 63
Valéry (P.), 29
Vansteenberghe (E.), 135
Vaux (A. de), 65

ANALYTICAL INDEX

A

Absolute, 44, 82, 83, 85
Act :
— and potency, 39, 42-46, 57-64, 83
— pure, 45, 57, 100
Action : divine, 106
Agape, 110, 111
Agnostics, 25
Atheism, 119
Authentic knowledge, 82
Autonomy, 132
Awareness, 46, 99

B

Baptism, 67
Being, 11, 20, 83, 86, 93
— composite, 60
— creative, 54
— divine, 84
— meaning of, 36, 38
— one, 72
— principle of thought, 57
— pure, 56
— question of, 8
— redemptive, 54
— subsistant, 89
— foundation of all intelligibility, 38

C

Causality, 82
Cause, 10, 25-32, 38-40, 46
— divine, 107
— necessity for, 71
— notion of efficient, 43
— prime, 62, 77
Censures, 24
Charity, 112
Christ, 22, 33, 55, 67, 97, 112, 127, 134
Communication, 5
Communion, 110-112
— with God, 112
Comprehension, 5
Conscience, 24, 122
Contingency, 44
Covenant, 31-32, 66, 109
Creation, 22, 55, 105-106

D

Demonstration, 3, 41, 139
— nature of, 27
— point of departure for, 27
Dependency, 18
Destiny, 59, 132
Dialectic, 82
Dialogue, 93
Duration, 77

E

Effect, 28
Ens, meaning of, 85
Esse :
— *subsistens*, 61, 83, 101
— actuality of, 37
Essence, 39-40, 42-45, 70, 82
Eternity, 32-33, 73-78, 134
Evil, 119, 122, 124
Existence :
— existential actuality, 86
— identity of, 83
— mode of, 88
— of God, 5, 20, 27, 60
Existents, 44, 59, 69, 76, 82, 87
Extension, 5, 58

F

Faith, 1-4, passim
Fideism, 25
Flesh and spirit, 52
Freedom, 132-133, 136

G

Gnostics, 24
Grace, 111, 129, 136-137

H

Habitus, 49
History and eternity, 73-75
— and Providence, 120-121
Human consciousness, 101
Human freedom, 106

I

Idea of God, 19-20
Identily, 30, 115
Idolatry, 23-24
Immanence, 100
Immateriality, 100
Immortality, 126
Incarnation, 55, 61-64
Innatism, 26
Intellect, 20, 46, 134

J

Judgment, 85-86
Justice, 112, 123-124, 138

K

Knowledge, 10, 17, 25, 37, 47-50, 81,
    87, 98-101, 139

L

Language, 5, 81
Law, 96
— natural, 122
Love, 54, 108-118, 138

M

Matter, 58-59, 98-99
Metaphysics, 10, 140
Modernism, 26
Motion, proof from, 42
Mystery, 138

N

Names, divines, 79
Negation, 82, 84

O

Ontological argument, 17, 20
Ontological distinction, 39

P

Pantheism, 55-56, 61-64
Perfection, 52-55, 60-61
Polytheism, 64
Potency, 42, 58, 77, 82, 133
— see Act
Predestination, 125-138
Providence, 118-125

R

Reason, 18, 20, 63, 132
Redemption, 123
Reprobation, 128-131
Revelation, 4-11, 88-89

S

Salvation, 127
Sanctity, 52-55, 125
Simplicity of God, 52-64
Sin, 122, 124, 136-138
Spirit, 52-58
Stoics, 128
Subsistence, 83
Substance, 56
Suffering, 119, 124

T

Theodicy, 1-11, 88-89, 139-141
Theology, 1-11, 88-89, 139-141
Thought :
— divine, 102
— Hebrew, 32
— subsistent, 101
Time, 16-18
Tradition, 55
Trinity, 109-112, 116, 140-141
Truth, 41

U

Unicity, 65, 72
Union, hypostatic, 55-56
Unity :
— experience of, 69
— of being, 70, 72
— of God, 64-73
— reason for, 69

V

Vision, of God, 16
Volition, in God, 105-108, 115, 122

W

Will, 45, 105
— see Volition; Freedom

Y

Yahweh, 31, 53, 65-67, 74, 96

NY. 42. — Printed in Belgium by Desclée & Co, Éditeurs, S. A., Tournai — 10.956

D—1969—0002—4